How to Manage Money

Building Your Business
Other titles in this series are:

Know Your Law
by Greville Janner QC MP

How to Manage People
by Ron Johnson

How to Win Profitable Business
by Tom Cannon

For details see back of book

How to Manage Money

G. D. Donleavy and
M. Metcalfe

Business Books
London Melbourne Sydney Auckland Johannesburg

Business Books Ltd
An imprint of the Hutchinson Publishing Group
17-21 Conway Street, London W1P 6JD
Hutchinson Group (Australia) Pty Ltd
30-32 Cremorne Street, Richmond South, Victoria 3121
PO Box 151, Broadway, New South Wales 2007
Hutchinson Group (NZ) Ltd
32-34 View Road, PO Box 40-086, Glenfield, Auckland 10
Hutchinson Group (SA) (Pty) Ltd
PO Box 337, Bergvlei 2012, South Africa
First published 1984

Set in Helvetica
Printed in Great Britain by The Anchor Press Ltd
and bound by Wm Brendon & Son Ltd
both of Tiptree, Essex

British Library Cataloguing in Publication Data
Donleavy, G. D.
How to manage money
1. Business enterprises-Finance
I. Title II. Metcalfe, M
658.1'5 HG4026

ISBN 0 09 151820 2 (cased)
0 09 151821 0 (paper)

Building Your Business

Series Editor: Tom Cannon

The last decade has witnessed a growing awareness of the importance of a healthy small business sector. The individuality, flexibility and creativity of the entrepreneur are recognized as vital to economic prosperity. Yet the same period has thrown up more and more challenges to the small firm. Competition has become more rigorous, while the need for efficiency and the effective application of resources has increased sharply. Perhaps the most valuable of these resources today is knowledge.

This series of books has been designed specifically for the entrepreneur, to bring to the owner and manager of the small firm vital areas of knowledge and information. The aim throughout has been to break down the barriers between theory and practice. The books are 'action-oriented' and this action-orientation is built into the texts themselves. Each book is broken down into self-contained Units. Each Unit sets out **Key Issues**, develops the issues and ends with **Action Guidelines**. Wherever possible, examples are drawn from the actual experience of small business people. Each author is an expert in his own field but equally at home with the application of his expertise to the small firm.

Growing recognition of the needs of the small firm has led to a range of initiatives to provide assistance. Government at a national and local level, large companies, banks and voluntary agencies are actively seeking ways to help the owner and manager of the small business to thrive. However the key characteristic of this type of company is its dependence on individual effort and skill. The onus for survival and prosperity lies on the man or woman who turns these ideas into action.

This series focuses on the key areas of customers, money, people and the law. The ideas presented will help provide the management expertise which leads to success.

Contents

Preface

You have begun to read this book because you and the authors are both concerned to achieve one thing more than anything else. That is *your success in business.* What you want to find are practical guidelines for managing the profitability of your firm. You want to be able to understand what you read straight away. You do not have the time or the inclination to plough through jargon, technicalities and out-of-date rules. For this reason, practical methods of working are set out, and detail in such rapidly changing areas as tax and law, where today's rules are so often tomorrow's waste paper, is purposely kept to a minimum.

This book is about accounting, costing and finance as they affect small businesses. It is not a textbook. It does not cover all aspects of these subjects. It assumes that you the reader have no special knowledge of these areas but that you do understand the facts of business life.

The book offers

- practical methods of handling your books and accounts so that you have a readily available thermometer of your firm's temperature, a regular and frequent picture of your profitability and, financially speaking, you can see yourself as others see you
- guidance on cost control as the necessary basis for sound and profitable pricing policies
- guidelines on financial planning and control by means of soundly based, realistic budgets that establish your targets for the coming year, so you know where you are heading.

The question of money itself is discussed and advice is offered for minimizing the difficulties associated with its seemingly eternal scarcity.

You do not have to read the entire book. Look at the contents page and carefully select the units you want. If there is still some doubt then turn to the 'Your problem' pages. Here is a general guide:

Retailers: Units 10, 14, parts of 11, and 15 will be of no use to you. When book-keeping you will not need a work-in-progress or a finished goods stock account.

Service industries: Unit 14, except for the last section, will be of little interest. This is also true of some parts of Units 10 and 11.

Jobbing companies: This term, I hope not ungraciously, has been used to include builders, engineers who make things to order, tailors, garage servicing and upholsterers - in fact anyone who makes things to special order.

The subject of TAX is not really covered by this book, although references are made to it under the subjects of managing costs and paying the owner.

VAT is covered, not comprehensively but enough for most firms to feel they might attempt to send in a return.

The use in this book of separate units each aimed at solving one type of problem should prove particularly attractive to owners of small businesses.

Your Problem

Your problem —— go to ——> Unit No

Your problem	Unit No
A Threatening Bank Manager	15 Controlling Your Working Capital 8 Have You Done Well?
A Massive Growth Anticipated	15 Controlling Your Working Capital 8 Have You Done Well? 16–18 The Management of Capital
You do not understand the terminology	2 Do You Understand the Language?
You wish to reduce the Accountant's bill	3–9 Book-keeping 16 Dealing with the Bank
Costing and Pricing	10 Costings 11 Pricing
Budgeting – how many should I make?	14 Budgeting 11 Pricing
What profit *will* I make?	10–15 Planning and Control
What profit *have* I made this month?	3–9 Book-keeping
How much cash will I need?	15 Controlling Your Working Capital

Question	See
Should I buy that asset?	13 Buying Fixed Assets
How much have I earned for myself?	18 Drawings and Valuations
Should I buy that company?	8 Have You Done Well? 13 Buying Fixed Assets 18 Drawings and Valuations
What do I do about the bank?	16 Dealing with the Bank
VAT	9 VAT
Where can I get money from?	17 Evaluating Money Sources
Do I do enough accounting?	1 Reviewing Your Situation
Inflation?	15 Controlling Your Working Capital 18 Drawings and Valuations
How much can I borrow?	8 Have You Done Well? 18 Drawings and Valuations 17 Evaluating Money Sources

Look carefully at the contents page for other areas of interest.

Section I

Introduction

1

Reviewing Your Situation

- **A lack of good accountancy is a primary cause of business failures.**
- **You should be able to measure any firm's solvency, its profitability, its return on capital employed, and its 'potential'.**
- **There is more to accountancy than book-keeping and tax calculations.**

Many small businesses fail

Why? Not because of the rate of inflation, interest rates, or the world recession, but because of *ignorance.*

Ignorance of the company's performance compared with that of competitors.
Ignorance of costs.
Ignorance of the sources of money.
Ignorance of the right sort of money to use in a particular situation.
Ignorance of the firm's liabilities and resources.

If you want your company to fail you need do no more than say: 'I keep it all in my head; accountants are parasites; who needs records?; planning is a waste of time' – and then wait awhile!

Managers of healthy firms have a healthy respect for knowledge, and this includes knowledge of the financial position of the firm.

If you are just starting or about to expand a business, if you are a retailer, a wholesaler, a jobbing manufacturer, a mass production firm, or in the service industry, you will *need* detailed knowledge.

You will need to know:

- your income and expenditure
- how to understand all your, and your debtors', various financial statements
- how to price your product or service
- how to forecast your future profits and cash requirements
- how much you must sell to achieve your profit target
- where and when you should look for extra money
- whether a machine or building is worth buying or leasing
- how many labour hours will be involved for a given level of sales

Also, you must be able to recognize *overtrading, undertrading, undercapitalization, overhead acceleration, whether you can afford a 10 per cent pay rise for your employees,* and *how much money you can afford to draw out of the firm's profit for yourself.*

If you cannot do any of the above you need this book.

Accountancy was born out of necessity, *the necessity to know what is going on.* A good small business manager is part production manager, part marketing manager, part maintenance man *and* part accountant.

Twenty questions

Here are twenty questions about your business. Only *you* can answer those in Part 1 – those in Part 2 are answered at the end of the questions. If you score more than eight in each part of the quiz, you might not need this book. If you score less than eight, on the other hand, you should benefit from this book. The test? After reading the book and applying its methods, you should be able to return to this quiz, and score eight or more in each part.

Part 1

1. How much cash in the bank does your business have right now?
2. How long do your customers take to pay your invoices on average?
3. How big was your net profit or loss last month?
4. How many months is it between now and your next phone bill?
5. *Precisely* how much net profit do you make on every article you sell (or hour of service rendered, as the case may be) after taking all overheads into account?
6. What is your forecast net cash flow this month?
7. What is the equity in your firm's assets?
8. What was your working capital at the end of last month?
9. How much did you withdraw from your business last month?
10. What is your weekly total labour cost?

Part 2

1. Return on capital employed measures a firm's:
   (*a*) solvency (*b*) profitability (*c*) profit
   (*d*) creditworthiness?
2. Overheads are, in the main:
   (*a*) variable costs (*b*) fixed costs (*c*) direct costs
   (*d*) capital expenditure?
3. When a firm receives a cheque for £300 from a debtor, X Ltd, the account that will be credited is:
   (*a*) cash (*b*) sales (*c*) X Ltd (*d*) profit and loss?
4. If a firm purchases a new machine for £5000, then:
   (*a*) its profit falls by £5000 (*b*) its working capital falls by £5000 (*c*) its working capital rises by £5000 (*d*) its overdraft must rise by £5000?

5 Only one of the following statements is true. Which one?

(*a*) If a firm makes a profit, it cannot be in danger of being liquidated.

(*b*) If a firm's product is in demand, at profitable prices, it cannot fail.

(*c*) If a firm owes to creditors more than it has in the bank, it must fail.

(*d*) If a firm can pay its debts as they fall due, it will be able to survive.

6 If a firm has overheads of £1000 per month, makes one product which cost £53 each to make (excluding the overheads) and the sales forecast is for between 100 and 120 per month, the overhead absorption rate is:

(*a*) 10 per cent (*b*) £10 per item (*c*) £9.10 per item
(*d*) can't be calculated?

7 The basic material cost per product is £7, all other costs add a further £16. If material losses of 5 per cent and production losses of 2 per cent are now to be allowed for, the unit cost is:

(*a*) £23 (*b*) £24.61 (*c*) £23.817 (*d*) £23.49?

8 A firm has £5000 worth of outstanding debts and its annual credit sales are £30,000. This means that customers take an average time to pay of:

(*a*) 6 months (*b*) half a month (*c*) 2 months (*d*) 3 months?

9 How many of its product must a firm sell if it wants to make a profit of £9000, if its selling price is £20, its overheads are £17,000 and other costs are £12 per item:

(*a*) 3250 (*b*) 750 (*c*) 450 (*d*) 1125?

10 A man's tax code is 312, the income tax rate is 30 per cent, NHI is 6 per cent on gross and his gross pay is £150 per week. What will his take home pay be:

(*a*) £114 (*b*) £54 (*c*) £96 (*d*) £127?

Answers to Part 2:

1 (*b*) profitability; return on capital employed = $\frac{\text{profit}}{\text{capital}}$

2 (*b*) fixed costs; these don't vary with the level of production

3 (*c*) X Ltd; a credit entry against a debtor balance
4 (*b*) cash decreases or creditors increase; fixed assets increase
5 (*d*) profits are not cashflows
6 (*d*) need an exact sales forecast
7 (*c*) [£7 × 1.05) + £16] × 1.02 = £23.817
8 (*c*) $\frac{£5000}{£30,000} \times 12 = 2$ months
9 (*a*) Overheads + (other cost × N) + profit = selling price × N
£17,000 + (12 × N) + 9000 = 20 × N
$N = \frac{26,000}{8} = 3250$
10 (*a*) [£150 – (£90 × 30%)] – £9 = £114

Knowing the key financial aspects of your business

It might be a bit of a shock for some to discover how little they know about the *financial* aspects of their own business. Others might have decided that the questions were irrelevant and not bothered to do them. If you are one of these people, think again. The purpose of the quiz was to establish what you now know about some *key* aspects of your business's financial position.

The questions in Part 1 of the quiz are designed to see:

- if you have your finger on your firm's pulse
- if you are steering your firm through the traffic of the business world with an eye open for traffic signals
- if you have so organized your time as to allow you to see the whole picture at least once a month

A firm that knows its monthly profit appreciates its monthly performance.

A firm that knows its cash position knows its safety margin.

These things are surely too important to be left entirely to your book-keepers and accountants.

Why the questions in Part 2?

Some of these are inevitably describing situations you and your firm may never meet. The answers are:

- You *will* meet situations where identical skills are required to the ones tested in those questions.
- You *will* need to price ahead of inflation.
- You *will* need to produce beyond your break-even volume when you make any product.
- You *will* need to know what does and what does not trigger liquidations: if not of your firm, then of a defaulting customer.

You may not need to outpace union wage negotiators, but you may need to renegotiate a cost-plus contract where the principles are very similar. In short, you will need certain basic financial and accounting skills to steer your business to profitable growth. Your accountant can and should help but it is *you* who have to make the decisions. Only those practical techniques that are *directly relevant* to making business decisions are included in this book.

What can business get from accounting and finance?

Accounting is the art of providing accurate information, in an understandable manner, in order to help improve the profitability of business decisions. Accounting data revolves around twin poles –

one is to do with profits as the dynamo of growth

the other is to do with cash as the foundation of survival.

This twin polarity is basic. It gives rise to a fundamental maxim, namely: *making money is not the same thing as making profits.*

Accountancy focuses on profit but includes money. Finance focuses on money but includes profit. Financial management means controlling the firm's whole structure of assets and liabilities, not just the cash. As such, finance is a *key* aspect of every other sort of management. Every manager therefore needs to appreciate the role of finance in his business – survival depends on it.

Accounting improves business decisions

It must be admitted straight away that accounting is more useful in some areas than in others. Accounting is very important in the following decision situations:

- at what price to sell the firm's output
- what type of proposals will be most persuasive to a potential backer or lender
- whether to make or buy a component part
- whether to lease, buy or acquire on hire-purchase a new machine
- which of several alternative investments is likely to be the best value
- whether the firm's performance is ahead of inflation (and/or that of competitors) enough to attract new funds, and how to attract such funds
- whether it is worth while to diversify out of an old product line into a new one
- whether an idea for saving costs or increasing sales will really raise profits after all relevant changes are taken into account.

These decisions are dealt with in the following pages. However, accounting is not very useful in making the following business decisions:

- whether to recruit Smith or Jones
- whether Birmingham or Manchester represents the more promising new market
- whether a particular new machine will raise productivity enough to be worth while (this is a production management problem although accounting can spell out what 'worth while' means in this context)
- whether consumers will be very sensitive or relatively indifferent to a proposed price rise.

While accounting may not be very useful in deciding what to do in these four situations, it is useful in *measuring the effects* of such decisions on profits once the decision has been taken.

Accounting is the basic language of business

We can see, then, that accounting helps in many vital decisions in business but not in all of them. However, it is more than an aid to decisions: it is also the basic language of business life. A little anecdote will help make this point.

A famous Chairman of a large public company was lying in bed reflecting on his day at the office. His wife was trying to get to sleep but had too little room in the bed to get comfortable. 'Turn over,' she snapped to her husband. '£3,516,544 and 52 pence' came the immediate response.

That is how accounting is the language of business.

The key words are: profit, overheads, margins, return on capital employed and break-even point. Success in business may be symptomized by a big house, a luxurious or fast car and exotic holidays, but it is measured by accounting reports, in particular by the profit shown on the profit and loss account and by the capital employed shown on the balance sheet.

The relationship between these two reports is shown by one figure above all, a figure that is widely held to be the single most important gauge of business performance - the return on capital employed (ROCE). It is found by dividing the net profit by the capital employed shown on the balance sheet. More precisely still, it is the net profit before interest and tax are deducted, divided by fixed assets plus working capital. The resultant percentage tells us whether our money and that of our backers would have shown a better return from a bank deposit account, a building society or some other sort of investment.

In other words, our ROCE tells us how our firm performs *as an investment.* A firm with an ROCE below the rate of inflation is not really profitable at all, because in *real* terms (i.e. after accounting for inflation) such a firm has operated at a loss. Real business growth comes from real profits, and real profit percentages begin where inflation rate percentages end. ROCE is so important that it is sometimes called the *primary ratio.*

How to calculate ROCE

XY Ltd	£		£
Sales	3,505	Fixed assets	8,000
Costs	2,505	Current assets	5,000
Net profit	1,000	Total tangible assets	13,000
Interest	200	Current liabilities	3,000
Taxable profit	800	Net tangible assets	10,000
Tax	400	Goodwill	2,000
Earnings	400	Net assets	12,000

In the left-hand block the figure we are interested in is £1000 for net profit, as it is before interest and tax. In the right-hand block the net assets of £12,000 include goodwill of £2000 which is not really representing a concrete physical asset, so it is ignored in ROCE calculations. The net assets we want to represent the capital employed are the net tangible assets of £10,000 because that is the true productive capital base.

$$\text{ROCE} = \frac{\text{net profit}}{\text{net tangible assets}} = \frac{1000}{10{,}000} = \frac{1}{10}$$

Profits are one tenth of capital, i.e. 10 per cent. If inflation is zero, an ROCE of 10 per cent is good; but if inflation is, say, 15 per cent, then an ROCE of 10 per cent is very unsatisfactory indeed.

Action Guidelines

1 Go through the 'contents' page of this book crossing off what you do or know about already.

2 Select the remaining parts that interest you and go through them, if necessary, with a calculator at hand. You might start with the terminology.

3 Follow up any unanswered questions you have by, for example, going to your local college library, telephoning the School of Accounting at the college, asking your accountant or asking your friends.

4 At work always concentrate on what you are going to do rather than what you have done. However, keep checking your plans against what actually happened. This will help improve your future plans.

5 Make sure all your present financial forms and papers are all seen by you and are filed neatly away for easy access later.

2

Do You Understand the Language?

- **What is meant by the cost of something as opposed to its price?**
- **What is the difference between an accrual and your creditors?**
- **Accountants and bankers have clearly defined meanings for words. Are they the same as yours?**

There are some basic words and phrases you need to know. Read through the following explanations even though you may think you know what the terms mean.

Costs (see Unit 10)

You pay out for *costs*, customers pay you the *price*. Costs include materials, labour and overheads. Salaries are one type of overhead, electricity, rents and stationery are others. It is all right to say 'my overhead costs'.

Costs + profit margin = selling price.

The Institute of Cost Accountants defines material costs as

price × quantity

because if, for example, you are building a house, the brick material cost is the price you paid per brick (say 8p) multiplied by the number of bricks it will take to make the house, say 10,000. Thus the brick cost is £800.

Variable costs These (as used here) vary according to your level of production. If your firm is closed for a holiday or a strike it will not consume variable costs. In this book we have assumed that the only variable costs are materials and some packaging overheads.

Fixed costs These include most overheads, and they have to be paid even if nothing is produced or sold. They vary with time. Examples are rent and salaries. Labour is treated as a fixed cost.

The best way to determine your variable costs is to examine each cost and ask yourself 'does this cost vary in direct proportion to the quantity I make or sell'.

Profit margin (Unit 11)

This means profit per unit. It is quite possible to have a very high profit margin without the firm actually making a profit. Why is that? Well, imagine we are the producer of a newspaper. The unit cost of our newspaper might be 10p per copy. We might have a dubious sales policy and charge £1 for the newspaper; this means we could have a profit margin of 90p. Soon we may find that nobody buys the paper, so that we have no sales income. We have a profit *margin* of 90p because that is merely a pricing matter. But we have no *profit* because we have made no sales! High profit margins do not by any means guarantee high profits, unless they can be realized.

Profit margin is often stated as a percentage of the *sales* value. *Mark-up* can be the same cash amount as the profit margin but is a percentage of the *cost.*

Profit (see Unit 7)

Simply stated, profit equals sales minus costs. We have to be careful here because some costs, like those of machines, are incurred one year and the items used in later years. This is overcome by use of a cost called *depreciation.*

Some costs may not yet have actually been paid for, but must be included as costs before your profit can be calculated. These unpaid costs are called *accruals.*

Profit can be either *gross profit* or *net profit*, much as wages can be 'gross' or 'net':

		or		
Gross wages	£100		Gross profit	£1000
Less deductions	£20		*Less* overheads	£900
Net wages	£80		Net profit	£100

For net profit, the deductions are overheads. The term gross profit is rather old-fashioned and used mainly by non-manufacturing firms, such as retailers.

Corporation tax may be deducted from the net profit, to give *net profit after tax.* There is also the concept of *retained profit.* This is the profit kept in the business after all payments to the owners of the business, drawings and dividends in particular, have been taken out. The retained profits are also often called *ploughed-back profits*, because the money is used to expand the firm by buying new assets.

An account (see Unit 3)

An account is a record of one particular type of transaction. So if on one page of a book you keep a record of all your electricity bills and payments this will be your electricity account. If on another page you record what you owe to Mr T. Smith, that will be Smith's account.

Profit and loss account (see Unit 7)

This is the *report* which shows the calculation of the profit (gross, net and retained). A brief example of a profit and loss account is shown in Table A.

The basic profit and loss account begins with sales revenue and goes down to net profit. In the last part of the account, the appropriation section, it goes from *net* profit to *retained* profit. In

Table A
Simple profit and loss account

	£	£	£	
Sales revenue			500,000	
Opening stocks of materials	50,000			
Materials costs	200,000			
Less Closing stock of materials	60,000			
Material costs		190,000		
Factory wages		40,000		
Electricity		20,000		
Selling costs		25,000		
Office costs		25,000		
Advertising		25,000		
Interest on loans		25,000		
			350,000	
Net profit before tax			150,000	Appropriation section
Taxation			60,000	
Net profit after tax			90,000	
Drawings			20,000	
Retained profit			70,000	

book-keeping, the profit and loss account, often abbreviated to P&L Account, is a *final* account of the books. That means that the profit and loss account represents a summary of all the other accounts, and therefore must be prepared last.

Not all the accounts kept by your firm will be summarized in the profit and loss account - an example is the record (account) of your overdraft balance. These accounts are usually called capital accounts because, when totalled, they result in a figure which corresponds to the firm's capital. They are also recognizable as items not directly used in the manufacture of the firm's products. These accounts are summarized in the *balance sheet.*

The costs in the P&L account are called *revenue* costs, as opposed to *capital* costs (such as those of machines) which go into capital accounts, to be later depreciated into the P&L account.

Balance sheet (see Unit 7)

The balance sheet is a list of the assets and liabilities of the business at a certain date. The assets of the business are the business's resources. Assets may be *fixed*, *current* or *intangible*. The *fixed* or *permanent* assets are land, buildings, plant, machinery, furniture, fixtures and fittings. *Current,* or short-term, assets are stocks, debtors, cash and petty cash and, in some businesses, investments on the Stock Exchange as well.

Intangible assets are those like customer relationships, copyrights, patents, and know-how which the firm may have paid something for if it was purchased as a going concern, presumably on the grounds that they would be an asset to the business, but which do not have a real physical existence in the sort of way that cash, land, buildings or machinery do. Nevertheless, they do appear in the assets side of a balance sheet. The total value of these assets, less any debts or loans, is equal to the firm's *capital*, also called its *equity*.

Capital (see Unit 7)

Capital represents money put into the business by the owner of the business. The original money in the business is the capital in the business at first. If the firm retains any profits over the following years, those profits will add to the firm's capital (even if only kept as cash). In other words, after the first year of trading, capital consists of initial money put into the firm plus the retained profits for the year's trading. Profit retained belongs to the owners of the business.

On the company balance sheet one usually finds the terms *equity and profit retained reserves* or *capital accounts* – these represent the capital, that is the profits retained over the years, plus the original capital.

Liabilities (see Unit 7)

Debts, or liabilities, are another source of money, much like capital or profits. Liabilities come in two forms, *deferred* and *current.*

Deferred, or long-term, liabilities principally consist of loans made to the business by banks, by the public at large or even possibly by the founder of the firm.

When a sole trader (owner manager) puts some money into his firm he can elect to call it 'capital' or a 'loan'. If he declares the latter, it is recorded as a *deferred liability.*

Deferred taxation represents tax that will have to be paid in over a year's time. The idea of tax being a loan is a little hard to swallow. However, the liability to pay the tax has occurred, so it is only through the generosity of the taxman(!) that the firm is allowed to retain the money for a while. Whilst the firm is being 'loaned' the money it can use it to run the business.

Current liabilities

These may consist of debts due for repayment in the near future (creditors), money received for some future service (e.g. for season tickets), or accruals, i.e. a reserve for unpaid bills.

Current liabilities also include *current taxation*, that means tax which is due to be paid within one year.

Often also found under current liabilities is the entry *overdraft.* Banks give overdrafts *and* bank loans, but the two things are not identical. An overdraft means a sum borrowed from the bank up to, not exceeding, a maximum amount – thus the size of the overdraft used can vary daily. A *bank loan,* which is a long-term loan or deferred liability, is a fixed sum borrowed for a fixed period, although repayment can be at any time. After repayment new loans may be negotiated. More importantly, the bank can demand repayment of an overdraft at very short notice even when a business has used its overdraft facility correctly year after year. Hence an overdraft is always a current liability while a bank loan is usually a deferred liability.

Balance sheet equation

The balance sheet is subject to the so-called balance sheet equation. That means that the total of the monies used by the firm must be accounted for in its assets. Thus, the balance sheet equation is: capital plus liabilities = assets.

It is worth remembering that the balance sheet was the original accounting document which investors demanded to ensure that managers were using the money given to them correctly. In the example shown in Table B the firm has £300,000 for the running of the business and the right hand columns show *how* this £300,000 is being used at that point in time.

Table B
Simple balance sheet

Capital	£	£	**Assets**	£	£
Initial investment	30,000		Fixed assets		
Profit retained	70,000		Buildings	100,000	
			Machinery	60,000	
		100,000	Furniture	25,000	
Deferred liability					185,000
Loan from IC bank		60,000			
Current liabilities			*Current assets*		
Creditors	40,000		Stocks	60,000	
Current tax	60,000		Debtors	50,000	
Bank overdrafts	40,000		Cash on hand	5,000	
		140,000			115,000
		300,000			300,000

Value

This is not really an accounting term at all - it is more of an economic or emotive term! Nobody has yet found an objective, generally agreed method of measuring the value of an item. What I think to be good value, you may think to be atrocious. Value is a subjective judgement. It is not true to say that the cost of something represents its value. It is entirely a matter of personal opinion. Value, therefore, is a personal or subjective term, not an accounting term. Its use is, therefore, to be discouraged when talking about business decisions. You should rather talk about an item's 'purchase price', 'replacement price' or its present 'market price'.

Cash flow (see Unit 15)

Cash flow is an important item often encountered in business discussions these days. It means the flow of actual cash into or out of the business. It is therefore reflected in the firm's bank account and cash reserves. *Net* cash flow is the cash payments made less cash receipts - in other words, the amount of cash coming into or leaving the business.

Depreciation (see Unit 6)

Depreciation is an overhead cost shown in the profit and loss account to cover the cost of wear and tear of fixed assets, in particular, machinery. If a machine has a ten-year life and it cost £10,000 with no scrap value, it may be said to depreciate by £1000 every year for ten years.

Depreciation allows the cost of a machine etc. to be transferred from an asset account into a cost against profit. The amount left, of the machine, to depreciate at any point in time should reflect the sales value of the machine. Therefore, depreciation means a fall in the resale value of the business, i.e. a reduction of the assets, and thus of the capital. It therefore serves to spread the cost of an expensive item evenly over its life. Depreciation affects profit but not cash flow.

Working capital (see Unit 15)

This is calculated by subtracting current liabilities from current assets. It shows us whether the firm is 'liquid' or not - that is, whether the firm is easily able to pay its debts without selling some fixed assets.

It is called *working* capital because it is that part of the firm's capital that is constantly changing from cash to stock to debtors to cash, again and again. It therefore consists of short-term (current) assets and liabilities.

Value-added

This is a relatively new term. Some people claim it is a better measure of business performance than profit. The government feel it is worth taxing (VAT)! If you buy materials, work on them and add a profit, you have increased their value. Value-added, then, is the difference between the sales value and the cost of materials and expenses purchased into the firm. What is 'added' consists of wages, salaries and profit – the 'internal' costs of the firm.

Drawings (see Unit 18)

Drawings are a very important part of business vocabulary, especially for the small businessman. Drawings mean anything taken out of the business by its proprietor. It does not matter whether it is cash, petrol on the firm's account, food, entertainment or anything else that the proprietor takes out of the business for his own personal use – if it is not *clearly* a genuine business expense, it is a drawing. Of course it is possible to argue that all sorts of things, for example, a subscription to the golf club, help business. So they might, but this argument could be extended indefinitely. For example, if a proprietor is feeling depressed one day because sales are not very good, he may argue that, in order to carry on that day, he needs several drinks at lunchtime. Is the cost of those drinks in the local pub a legitimate business expense? Psychologically yes, maybe, but for accounting purposes, and for the purpose of the Inland Revenue, *and* for the purpose of general and accepted business usage, the cost of such drinks is a drawing.

Drawings are a withdrawal of some of the profits of the firm. Advance drawings have to be carefully controlled. It is clearly quite possible for drawings to exceed profits, especially if you are unaware of your monthly profit level. Drawings, therefore, are a significant item which deserve, and will get, a chapter to themselves in this book.

Break-even point (see Unit 11)

An important term is the break-even point for each product. Assume a fixed selling price. If a firm produces too few items it will make a loss. If it makes more than a certain number of the items, it will make a profit. Between these two levels of output is an output volume which will cause the firm to report zero profit. This latter output volume is called the *break-even volume.* The volume multiplied by the sales price gives *break-even revenue.*

Double-entry book-keeping (see Unit 3)

This is a term we shall be exploring in some depth in the next few chapters. Book-keeping itself means keeping records (accounts) of a firm's receipts and payments, in order to be aware of the value of its assets and liabilities. *Double-entry* book-keeping acknowledges that for every business transaction, two entries have to be made in the accounts - one to record a receipt (called a debit), and another to record an outgoing (called a credit). For example, if you buy a car, £5000 goes out (is credited), and you are in receipt of £5000 worth of car (is debited). If you total the debit entries, and subtract the total of the credit entries, the two should cancel out. This provides a useful check that you have recorded everything correctly.

Note that an outgoing can be merely the acknowledgement of a debt. For example, if you buy the car on credit, you would record - received (debit) a car £5000; outgoing (credit) an IOU of £5000.

The end result, of the total debits equalling the total credits, is seen in the balance sheet totals as the assets equalling the capital.

Return on capital employed

It is now time for *you* to attempt something. These explanations are all well and good, but where are they leading? In Tables C and D you will find copies of the published final accounts of Arsenal Football Club. You should now understand the reason for producing these two statements, and the meanings of the items listed.

Let us now imagine you have some money available and have thought of owning, for some reason, Arsenal. Would it be a better investment than just putting your money in a Building Society or in a Bank Deposit Account? Would the return on your investment be greater than the present rate of inflation? For convenience, let us further assume that inflation is running at 8 per cent a year and the Building Societies are paying 12 per cent before tax.

The figure you want to extract from Arsenal's accounts is its *return on capital employed* (ROCE). This is calculated by

$$\frac{\text{profit}}{\text{capital}} \times 100\%$$

Go ahead, find Arsenal's (ROCE) and decide if it is a worthwhile investment.

Table C

ARSENAL FOOTBALL CLUB LIMITED

Profit and loss account for the year ended . . .

	£	£
Football income		
Gate receipts – net		1,327,986
Broadcasting and television fees		15,610
Profits from programmes, handbooks and ground advertisements		107,443
Profits from Gunners Shop		17,696
Sales revenue		1,468,735
Overheads		
Transfer fees – net	59,005	
Players, management and staff	689,746	
Police, referees and gatemen	49,321	
Ground maintenance and expenses	385,134	
General expenses	88,918	
Depreciation	17,069	
Audit fee	1,000	1,290,193
Football profit		178,542
Other income		8,907
Profit before tax		187,449
Corporation tax		75,046
Profit after tax		112,403
Appropriations		Nil
Retained		£112,403

Table D
ARSENAL FOOTBALL CLUB LIMITED
Balance Sheet at . . .

	£	£
FIXED ASSETS		481,536
CURRENT ASSETS		
Stock	29,649	
Debtors and prepayments	214,946	
Cash at bank and in hand	242,785	
	487,380	
CURRENT LIABILITIES		
Season tickets	97,084	
Creditors and accruals	341,701	
Unclaimed dividends	1,002	
Corporation tax	61,400	
	501,187	
NET CURRENT ASSETS AND LIABILITIES		13,807
DEFERRED LIABILITIES		467,729
DEFERRED TAXATION		15,000
TOTAL NET ASSETS		£452,729
FINANCED BY:		
SHAREHOLDER'S CAPITAL		5,849
RESERVES		446,880
TOTAL CAPITAL EMPLOYED		£452,729

D. J. C. H. Hill-Wood
S. C. McIntyre — Directors
K. J. Friar, Secretary.

Answer. The profit figure required must be the one after tax, because this cost has to be paid before the owner receives anything. The capital figure you must take in the calculation must include the reserves (accumulated retained profit) because they are used to finance the assets.

We should therefore calculate the ROCE as follows:

$$\frac{\text{profit after tax}}{\text{capital employed}} = \frac{£112,403}{£452,729} \times 100 = 24.8\%$$

I cannot see the owners parting with the company for less than £452,729. They ploughed back the profits rather than taking them for themselves, and so will want recognition for this.

Action Guidelines

1 Find your firm's ROCE. To do this:

(*a*) Total all your assets, that is, find the cost of all your buildings, machines, fittings, stock, debtors, and add on your cash reserves (include only things you actually own).

(*b*) Deduct all you owe, that is what you owe, today, to your suppliers, the tax man, VAT, overdraft, etc. Do not include any long-term loans used to set up the firm. You now have your firm's *capital employed*.

(*c*) Find out how much *profit* you have made this year to date. If you do not know then find out how much profit you made in your last (accounting) year. This profit figure should be after tax but before drawings (or dividends). Tax is a controllable expense like any other.

(*d*) Divide your profit figure by your capital figure and multiply by 100. You now have your firm's ROCE.

2 Compare the ROCE you have just calculated with your ROCE two years ago. Also compare it with the ROCE of one of your competitors.

3 Go to your local library (better still a college library) and ask to see a set of published accounts for any firm. Read this and make sure you understand the terminology.

3

How is Book-Keeping Done?

- **A general ledger acts as a summary file.**
- **Book-keeping is just a filing system – the filing of numbers.**
- **Whenever you make a financial transaction there are *two* movements. You receive something and you give out something.**
- **Good evaluation and planning of your firm's performance needs reliable records.**
- **If you post all your transactions to one ledger it may soon become full.**

When record keeping, you have to be careful not to turn into a bureaucrat. On the other hand it is important that your suppliers and customers do not make a fool of you. If you do not have at least some records of what you owe, are owed, and what you have, then you will be dependent on these other people.

Just keeping invoices and cheque stubs may be all right for running a household, but, for a company, the pile soon becomes too much to handle.

A good compromise between bureaucracy and confusion is a simple set of company accounts. The most efficient way of keeping these is to use *double-entry book-keeping.* It's simple, but precise. In the seventeenth century it was described as the only perfect science because every record was nicely balanced with another.

How exactly is it done?

So you want to set up and keep your own accounts? Remember, 'knowledge is power'.

First buy a book with ruled lines, that is a *ledger.* Later, you may need another three. Most businesses use something with a good stout cover, so it can also be used as a coffee-cup stand!

Take one of the books and head successive double pages with the items we meet in a balance sheet and a profit and loss account. You want double pages with these headings:

1 **Capital account**
2 **Reserves (profit) account**
3 **P&L account**
4 **Loans account**
5 **Creditors account**
6 **Accruals account**
7 **Fixed assets - machines account**
8 **Fixed assets - fixtures account**
9 **Fixed assets - buildings account**
10 **Stock - raw materials account**
11 **Stock - finished goods account**
12 **Debtors account**
13 **Prepayments account**
14 **Cash-in-hand account**
15 **Bank account**
16 **Sales account**
17 **Cost of sales account**
18 **WIP account**
19 **Wages account**
20 **VAT account**
21 **Drawing account**
22 **Overheads account**
(You can sub-divide this into say electricity, rates, rent, etc. as you see fit - one page for each.)

Next you must put a large margin down the right and left sides of each double page. Head the six sections Date, Item, Debit, Date, Item, Credit. You should also number each double page, that is each account. The crease down the centre makes an obvious division between the two sides.

19		WAGES ACCOUNT			
Date	Item	Debit £	Date	Item	Credit £

You may find that when you go searching for a suitable ledger you are offered one which is especially designed, with a lot of the lines ruled in for you. These are fine. Such ledgers usually use a double line to imitate the centre crease of an ordinary book. You may even decide to use a card system instead of a book.

Some entries

Now we shall make some practice entries (postings) to our new general ledger. We shall first state a transaction, then tell you how to make the posting. After a while we shall leave you to it. Note that the DEBIT postings go in the left-hand section; the CREDIT postings go to the right.

Transaction 1: The firm buys a machine (a lathe) costing £3000 in cash, on 1st January 1984.

Explanation 1: The firm has (1) received (debit) a machine and (2) given out (credit) cash.

Posting 1: Debit machines account with £3000.
Credit cash account with £3000.

The machines account and the cash account in the general ledger will now look like:

7		MACHINES ACCOUNT			
Date	Item	Debit £	Date	Item	Credit £
1/1/84	1 Lathe	3000.00			

14			CASH ACCOUNT		
Date	Item	Debit £	Date	Item	Credit £
			1/1/84	1 Lathe	3000.00

Later, when you have only the machines account open, you may wonder how you paid for the machine, that is, where the credit posting went. An obvious way of including this information is to add a reference column. This will go next to the item column and contain the cash account number, in this case 14.

Transaction 2: Sell product (a hatch cover) for £150 cash, on 2nd January 1984.

Explanation 2: Received (debit) £150 cash, give out (credit) product as sales. You can't credit the finished goods stock account, because the stock is held at cost, but you sell at cost plus a profit margin.

Posting 2: Debit cash account, £150.
Credit sales account, £150.

Thus, your sales and cash accounts will look like:

16				SALES ACCOUNT			
Date	Item	Ref.	Debit £	Date	Item	Ref.	Credit £
				1/1/84	Hatch Cover	14	150.00

14			CASH ACCOUNT				
Date	Item	Ref.	Debit £	Date	Item	Ref.	Credit £
2/1/84	Hatch Cover	16	150.00	1/1/84	1 Lathe	7	3000.00

To save space we shall have to abbreviate the way we are showing these accounts. From now on we shall show what is called the T form only:

16	SALES ACCOUNT	
		£
	Hatch Cover	150.00

Don't forget the date (use 3/2/84) and reference.

Transaction 3: Buy materials (steel) worth £750 on credit terms from Mr Stainless.

Explanation 3: Received (?) materials, give out (credit) an IOU (usually, your word or signature or a goods-received note will act as the IOU).

Posting 3: Debit raw material stock account £750. Credit creditors account £750.00 (that's why they are called creditors).

Transaction 4: Transfer £7000 from your personal bank account to the firm's bank account. You declare this to be capital, not a loan.

Explanation 4: Received (debit) in firm's bank £7000, and give out an IOU (or rather an agreement) for £7000 worth of capital.

Posting 4: Debit bank account £7000. Credit capital account £7000.

Transaction 5: Pay off your supplier, Mr Stainless, the £750 from transaction 3, by cheque.

Explanation 5: Receive (debit) back the IOU.
Give out (credit) £750 from bank account.

Posting 5: Debit creditors for £750.
Credit bank for £750.

Transaction 6: Transfer £500 from firm's bank account to the cash box in the office.

Posting 6: You do it! (The answer is given further on.)

Transaction 7: The firm sells a flange for £35 to Mr Abbott, but allows him one month to pay.

Posting 7: Debit debitors (Mr Abbott) (this explains the term debtors).
Credit the sales account with £35.

Transaction 8: The firm pays the office cleaner, Mrs Kleen, £10 in cash.

Posting 8: Debit overhead account (you may decide to have a special overhead account for office cleaning).
Credit cash account £10.
(We, too, shall forget the income tax, for now!)

Transaction 9: The firm returns £10 of the steel purchased from Mr Stainless as faulty.

Posting 9: You do it.

Transaction 10: Mr Abbott (from transaction 7) pays the firm £11 in cash.

Posting 10: You do it.

Transaction 11: Mr Abbott pays the balance of what he owes the firm, less £2 that was agreed he could deduct if he paid on time.

Posting 11: Debit cash £22.
Debit the settlement discount account with £2.
Credit the debtor's account with £24.

Note the decision to open a new account, called the settlement discount account. You can have whatever accounts suit you. The more there are the clearer each one will be.

Answers to postings: Posting 6: debit cash account £500; credit bank account £500. Posting 9: debit creditors £10.00; credit raw materials stock account £10.00. Posting 10: debit cash £11.00; credit debtors £11.00.

Summary

What you should now have in your general ledger is as follows:

MACHINES ACCOUNT

	£		£
Lathe	3000.00		

CASH ACCOUNT

	£		£
Sale: Hatch cover	150.00	Lathe	3000.00
Bank transfer	500.00	Mrs. Kleen	10.00
Mr Abbott	11.00		
Mr Abbott	22.00		

RAW MATERIALS STOCK ACCOUNT

	£		£
Steel	750.00	Returns to Mr Stainless	10.00

CREDITORS ACCOUNT

	£		£
Mr Stainless	750.00	Mr Stainless	750.00
Returns to Mr Stainless	10.00		

SALES ACCOUNT

	£		£
		Hatch cover	150.00
		Flange	35.00

CAPITAL ACCOUNT

	£		£
		From self	7000.00

BANK ACCOUNT

	£		£
Capital from self	7000.00	Mr Stainless	750.00
		To cash	500.00

DEBTORS ACCOUNT

	£		£
Mr Abbott	35.00	Mr Abbott	11.00
		Mr Abbott	24.00

OFFICE CLEANING ACCOUNT

	£		£
Mrs Kleen	10.00		

SETTLEMENT DISCOUNT ACCOUNT

	£		£
Mr Abbott	2.00		

You will have different descriptions under 'items'. The idea of this column is to provide room for you to put any notes or comments that *you* feel are relevant.

The date and cross reference account numbers are important. I simply did not have room.

The rules of book-keeping are:

- **Receipts are debits**
- **Outgoings are credits**
- By convention debits are placed to the left of credits.

Practical problems

You will have noticed that if you sell and buy a large number of items through a large number of people, the cash, bank, debtors, creditors, sales and raw material stock accounts are very quickly going to become too big for your ledger. Meanwhile the capital, tax and finished goods stock accounts are hardly being used.

This is where the other three ledgers come in. It is frequently a good practical move to start by listing the creditors, debtors and cash postings in their own separate ledgers. Then, at each month end, the totals of the month's postings for each ledger can be posted in the general ledger. These general ledger accounts being posted with the totals are called *control* accounts. Thus, in the general ledger you will have a creditors control account which will contain little detail - just monthly totals.

Figures 1 and 2 show book-keeping systems for a very small firm and for a larger firm.

We shall look at the secondary ledgers in the next few units.

A journal

In some firms a book called the journal is kept, to record transactions in chronological order (as they occur) prior to

Figure 1 The book-keeping system for a very small firm.

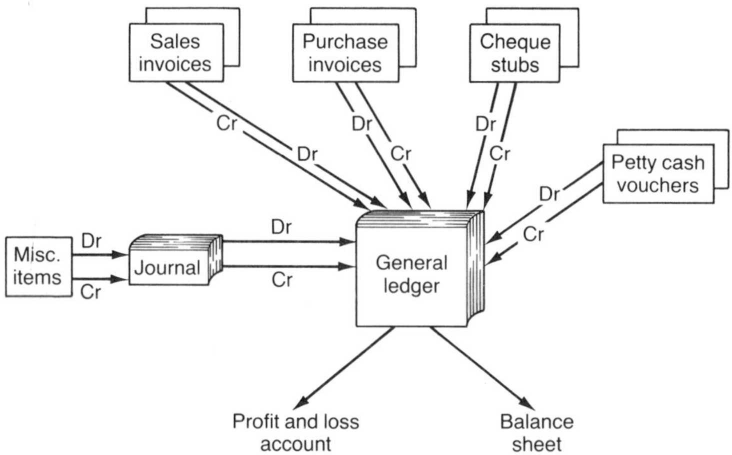

Figure 2 The book-keeping system for a larger firm.

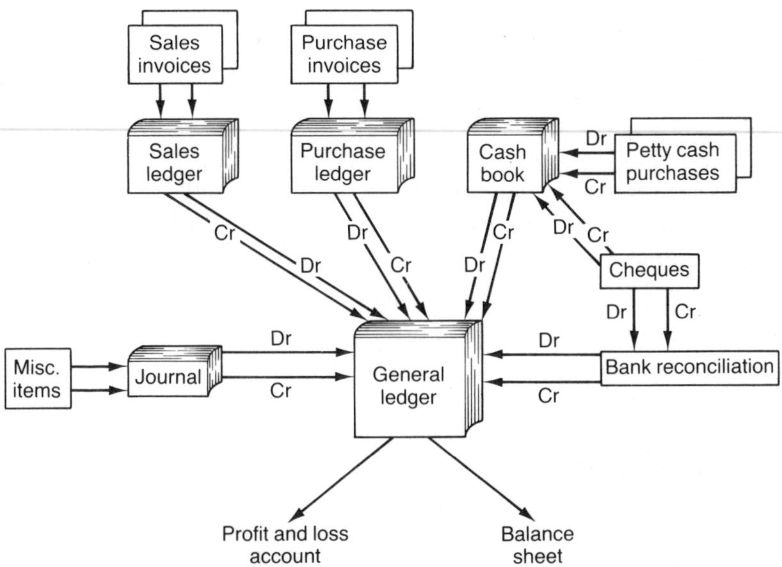

posting into the general ledger – so that you have a record of a day's activity and have more room for comments.

There is no doubt you can live without a journal. If you feel the need for a formal book to note special transactions that generate no documents of their own, then a journal can be used rather than endless scraps of paper. These postings in the journal are later written up in the general ledger. An example of a transaction which generates no documents is the scrapping of some rusty old fixtures which were originally recorded as assets. Another example is depreciation.

Starting point

Before you begin posting a month's transactions in your new general ledger, it will be necessary to record the firm's previous records. That is, the *opening* balance figures will have to be posted into the ledger. These opening balances include items like stock levels already in the firm, and capital already in the firm.

If you are about to start entering the accounts yourself, this is best done immediately after your accounting year-end. The auditor will have just prepared the balance sheet and the profit and loss account.

Posting the opening balances is simply a matter of writing the items shown on the *balance sheet* into the general ledger as 'opening balance'. Remember to debit your assets, and credit your liabilities, including capital and profit reserves (liabilities for the firm to pay the owners). Remember to check that when you add up all the debits and subtract the credits the total should be nil.

The profit and loss type accounts (e.g. overheads) will be empty, because they are annual expenditure records which are cleared to the P&L account at each year-end.

Making a start!

Remember, if you decide to keep fuller records and keep them yourself, you *can't* do any damage. In the first year you will still be learning, but you will only be recording *extra* information, so at worst you'll have some half-completed records and a few rather confused accounts. However, if you stick to the routine suggested in the next few units you won't go too far wrong.

If you keep these books you will save some of the expense of your auditor's fee, but more important you will have a simple but effective way of monitoring your firm's financial transactions.

Remember:

- If you file your financial transactions efficiently - that is if you keep books - you will have a lot of useful information. You will be able to use this information to make forecasts and thus decisions about the future.
- If you perform a financial transaction you alter two accounts. The first skill of book-keeping is to know which two and how. The second skill is to bother to record the alteration as soon after it has occurred as is reasonable.
- If you sell or buy a large number of small items per day then your ledgers will soon become enormous. The cash, debtor and creditor accounts will need to be summarized.

Action Guidelines

1 Whenever you conduct a transaction – for example, buy a car, loan money, buy stock, pay a bill – then:

(*a*) try to name the two accounts that will be affected by the transaction;

(*b*) try to determine which account is receiving (debit) and which is giving out (credit)

2 Ask stationery suppliers to show you their specialized accounting forms and books.

3 Get an attractive book-keeper to take over from you – it does so brighten up the office!

4

Recording Cash Transactions

- **Companies with few transactions may almost completely depend on the cashbook for their financial record keeping.**
- **Cash is the firm's life blood. It should be adequately controlled.**
- **Wages are a major cash transaction.**

The cash book

The cash and bank account ledgers will grow rather quickly if every transaction is posted separately. We shall now look at how we might allocate a book especially to cash transactions. Totals from this cash book will be posted to the general ledger.

Again take a blank ruled book. Head the first double page with today's date. Then rule up the columns as shown below. (You can have the crease where you like this time!)

Date: 1/3/83 *Reference*	*Total received*	*Total paid out*	*VAT*	*Drawings*	*Credit sales*	*Materials*	*etc.*	*Account?*	£
(1)	(2)	(3)	(4)	(5)	(6)	(7)	(8)	(9)	(10)

Column 1 This will contain the details of the transaction. These details may only need to be a signature.

Column 2 If you *receive* £150.00 cash for some reason, the £150.00 will appear here. Note that £150.00 includes VAT.

Column 3 If you *pay* £76.20 for some reason, for example, for beer, the £76.20 will appear in this column. Again it includes VAT. Any 'paid out' figures should be put in brackets. This will assist the adding-up later.

Column 4 The amount of VAT included in the entry in columns 2 or 3 will be entered here (it may be £0.00).

Column 5 If the cash paid out was for the private use of the owner, then the amount will be entered here.

Column 6 If the cash received was for credit sales (debtors), the amount, excluding VAT, is entered here. We will come back to this later. Cash sales are entered elsewhere. Note that the sum of the amounts in column 5 and column 4 equals that in column 3.

Column 7 If the cash paid out was for raw materials (not overheads), then the amount, less VAT, is entered here.

Column 8 Here you can enter the name of some other item that your firm receives or pays cash for on a regular basis. Examples are stationery and food. You must head this column as you feel appropriate. Initially you could leave it blank. If the column *is* headed, then there will need to be an identically named account in the general ledger.

Column 9 In this column you *name* the miscellaneous items of cash received or paid. For example, if you buy some stationery you would enter 'stationery' here. If you find the same name, 'stationery', appearing here regularly, you may set a special stationery column such as column 8. Note that the name used in column 9 will be used to post the general ledger later. The amount spent on stationery (excluding VAT) will be entered in column 10.

Column 10 See column 9 for details.

Some entries

Now that our new cash book is ready we ought to try some practice entries. *First* we must add up the amount in the firm's cash box or till, whichever it uses. Let us assume a *mainly* credit sale and credit purchase manufacturing company with a cash box in the firm's safe. The amount in the box is £150.00.

Transaction 1: Total present balance in cash box, £150.00.
Posting 1: In column 1: Opening balance.
In column 2: £150.00

Transaction 2: Clerk takes from the box £2.20 for stationery (exactly what she needs): £2.00 goods, £0.20 VAT. (The VAT is not based on real percentages.)

It seems a bit unsatisfactory that anyone can just take money from the box with no record of the reason! The simplest response to this is to say that the clerk should sign her name under 'reference' in the cash book. Does the owner feel he needs to approve the 'giving of money' *before* it is taken? If so, the book will have to be taken for his signature, before the cash is released. Alternatively, the owner can always sign a petty cash voucher as authorisation to take the money. The voucher number will be the reference.

Posting 2: In column 1: Signature/Voucher No.
In column 3: £(2.20).
In column 4: £(0.20).
In column 9: Stationery.
In column 10: £(2.00).

Transaction 3: You need some cash so that you can nip around the corner to buy a sheet of plastic. The plastic is needed to complete an order. It costs £41.45, the VAT an extra £3.90.

Posting 3: Paid out: £(45.35).
Reference: The invoice number, or order number or buyer's signature.
VAT: £(3.90).
Materials: £(41.45).

The receipt should have written clearly on it, 'in the cash book', dated 1/3/83, and then be put into a 'cash book documents' file.

Transaction 4: You receive four cheques in the post. They are all for sales, and total £403.60 for goods, plus £40.36 for VAT.

Posting 4: You now have to decide whether you want every cheque entered separately or the four batched together. Assuming you enter them separately (we'll only do one):
Reference: Customer's name.
Received: One cheque £70.73.
Sales: The goods' value £64.30.
VAT: The VAT value £6.43.

Transaction 5: You decide you need more cash in the box. You go to the bank and draw £200.00.

Posting 5: Reference: Cheque number.
Received: £200.00.
Account column: Bank.
£ column: £200.00.

Transaction 6: You take £100.00 for personal use.

Posting 6: Reference: Owner's signature.
Paid out: £(100.00).
Drawings: £(100.00).

Transaction 7: Daily cash sales money has been totalled from the till. Goods £750.01 plus VAT £75.00 are shown (and agreed by counting) on the till roll.

Posting: 7: Reference: Till roll 1/3/83 (this is filed).
Received: £825.01.
Account: Cash sales.
VAT: £75.00.
£: £750.01.

Transaction 8: You take potential overseas customer out for a meal. The bill comes to £27.07 which includes £2.46 VAT.

Posting 8: Reference: Owner's signature.
Paid Out: £(27.07).
VAT: £(2.46).
Account: Entertainment.
£: £(24.61).

Transaction 9: You decide to bank the excess in the cash box. The float is still to be £150.00.

Posting 9: Reference: Cashier's signature (file paying-in slip).
Paid out: £(921.12) (balance of other transactions).
Account: To bank.
£: £(921.12).

That should suffice to show how to use the cash book. If you made all the postings you should now have something like Table E. (Treat the brackets as minus signs.)

Table E
Date: 1/3/83

Reference	*Total received*	*Total paid out*	*VAT*	*Drawings*	*Credit Sales*	*Materials*		*Account?*	£
O. Balance	150.00								
J. Pretty		(2.20)	(0.20)					Stationery	(2.00)
Proforma 024376		(45.35)	(3.90)			(41.45)			
R. Customy	70.73		6.43		64.30				
Cheque 206304	200.00							From bank	200.00
M. E. Self		(100.00)		(100.00)					
Till roll	825.01		75.00					Cash sales	750.01
M. E. Self		(27.07)	(2.46)					Entertain.	(24.61)
J. Pretty		(921.12)						To bank	(921.12)
CLOSING BALANCE		(150.00)							
TOTAL	1245.74	(1245.74)	74.87	(100.00)	64.30	(41.45)			2.28

Postings

Next we shall consider how to post these figures to the general ledger. It would be normal policy to total-up, as shown, every day. The balances have to be carried forward. At the end of the month (as we shall assume it is for our nine postings), when you total-up, you will have the month's total, received and paid, plus a summary of what went on. The next month starts afresh with only the opening balance of £150.00.

So, with the general ledger, the cash book and a pen all together, postings can begin (see Figure 3). Numbers below in brackets are debited.

Figure 3 Transferring cash book totals.

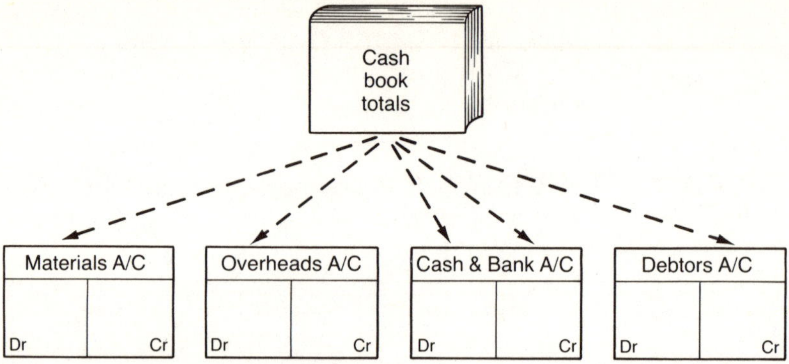

Postings: Debit 'Cash' £1,245.74
Credit 'Cash' £1,245.74

	£
Credit 'VAT account'	(74.87)
Debit 'Drawings account'	100.00
Credit 'Debtors account'	(64.30)
Debit 'Stock account'	41.45
Debit 'Stationery account'	2.00
Credit 'Bank account'	(200.00)
Credit 'Sales account'	(750.01)
Debit 'Entertainment account'	24.61
Debit 'Bank account'	921.12
	000.00

In the 'item' column of your general ledger you might enter 'Cash book' as the description. The balance on your cash account should agree with the balance in the cash book.

Wages routines

The Inland Revenue (hereafter the taxman!) says that the tax system in Britain is administered more cheaply than in any other country in the world. That's because you do it for them!

If you employ people, you take on a great responsibility on behalf of the taxman.

You have to record:

- the tax deducted this week and for the year to date
- the National Insurance (NI) deducted from the employee
- the NI *you* have contributed
- the employee's tax code and NI number.
- sick pay paid

The taxman has us all numbered from birth. Your child's birth certificate number is its NI number. If you correspond with the taxman, you will need to use this number because you are not unique enough for his nationwide files.

It is not possible to include here *all* the duties you have to perform for the taxman. Some jobs are for year-end returns, some are for employees changing jobs – there are many more. You must go to your local tax office and obtain their booklet P.7, *Employer's Guide to PAYE.* At the end of this book you will find a list of several of the taxman's publications.

We can, however, give you a *rough* idea of how tax deductions may be recorded. Remember that this is only illustrative of the principles involved, and that the tax office will give you the forms and routines.

You will need an employee's record card. This serves to record the wages paid and tax deducted. It will look something like the diagram below (you can buy special stationery).

Name: J. Abbott			Rate/hour: £2				Code: (1) ~~298H~~ (2) 301H		
	Hours	*Basic gross*	*Sick Pay*	*Total gross*	*Tax*	*Employee's NI*	*Cash*	*Employer's NI*	*Total*
This year This week	 40	 80	 20	2000 100	150 10	100 5	1750 85	120 7	2120 107
This year This week				2100	160	105	1835	127	2227
(1)	(2)	(3)	(4)	(5)	(6)	(7)	(8)	(9)	(10)

Column 1 Shows if the entry is for the year to date or just for this week.
Column 2 The hours J. Abbott has worked this week.
Column 3 The gross pay he has therefore earned at £2 per hour.
Column 4 The sick pay you have paid him on behalf of the DHSS.
Column 5 His basic pay plus sick pay.
Column 6 His tax liable on the 'Total gross' figure from column 5. This can be calculated from his code, but is best done using the *Tax Tables (Weekly Paid)* supplied by the taxman. The tables, in fact, give you the tax due this year to date.
Column 7 The employee's National Insurance contribution, again found from tables. National Insurance is for the Department of Health and Social Security, but the taxman will redirect it.
Column 8 The net pay - this is the amount in the pay packet. It is, of course, gross pay less tax and National Insurance.
Column 9 Employer's contribution to NI (from tables).
Column 10 The total cost of employing J. Abbott for that week. It is the total gross pay, plus the employer's contribution.

If you keep one of these cards for each employee, you can keep *one* as a 'totals' card at the front. You will then have a *wages control record.*

The book-keeping

When posted to the general ledger the postings will be (using J. Abbott's as the control card):

Debit: Wages account £107
Credit: PAYE tax account £10
Credit: Employee's NI £5
Credit: Employer's NI £7
Credit: Bank account £85 (if you draw a cheque to pay the wages).

Usually the bank will want to know how you want your cash - that is, how many £5, £1, 50p, 10p, 2p and 1p denominations. This you will have to work out from each wage record.

The entries above will be made once a week for each week in a month. Within fourteen days of the end of each month the taxman will want two cheques for

the tax deducted that month
the National Insurance deducted.

For use at the end of the year the taxman has another form which enables you to match your cheque payments with each employee's tax and NI deductions.

- A very small firm may not need to keep separate creditors and debtors' records. It may have just a cash book. Into this will go *all* the income and expenditure records.
- A good cash book will help with your book-keeping and may even consist of eighty per cent of it. It is an easy but useful filing system.
- The wages routine must be done to the taxman's rules, and on his forms. This is one area where a home computer might help.

Action Guidelines

1 Make sure that you obtain bank statements as frequently as you can, if only to see the balance.

2 From your records work out:

(*a*) whether overall your cash flow last month was into or out of the bank;

(*b*) what percentage of your sales income was from credit sales;

(*c*) what your largest item of expenditure was.

3 Make sure you know all the tax rules relevant to your business. If you are in any doubt whatsoever, visit your local tax office for free advice, or study the appropriate Inland Revenue leaflet.

5

How much are you owed; do you owe?

- **If the number of purchases and sales transactions is large you may be wise to record these in separate ledgers.**
- **Purchase and sales ledgers provide records of your credit taken and credit given**
- **It is essential to know day by day how much you are owed by whom, *and* how much you owe and to whom.**
- **Full use should be made of bank statements for checking purposes.**

Purchase ledger

You buy, on credit, from your creditors.

When a purchase invoice arrives in the post *it should be attached to its corresponding delivery note.* If no delivery note exists, but you agree that the invoice should be paid, then dating and initialling the back will suffice.

A purchase invoice is classified under the month in which the goods were delivered. (Beware the supplier who pre-dates deliveries.) So, if goods are delivered, or a service used, between 1st and 31st January, the associated invoice will be recorded as a January invoice. This is important not just from the accounting record angle, but so that you may know exactly when the invoice is due for payment. As most trade credit terms are 'end of the month following', we shall assume that here.

You will have to decide if it is worth checking the addition, etc. on your invoices; it seems a bit like a 'belt *and* braces' job to us!

Now for your purchase ledger. (It is also called the 'bought ledger' by some.) Whilst you can use another plain ruled book, it may be wise to go for a (lightweight) card system this time. These cards will need to be big (say 1 foot or 30 cm across). The advantages of cards are that in an alphabetical file (1) new names can easily be added, and (2) when an account is full a second card can easily be added.

Filling out cards So, leave your first card for now and head the second as follows, with the account name reflecting the heading of your purchase invoice:

Account: J. ABBOTT AND SONS (2) Tel: 061-212 43976 Address: 18 Hore Road M1R 5QT

Delivery date	Invoice no.	Balance c/f	Total	Stock	VAT	General ledger account?	£	Chq. no.	Chq. £
Jan. 83	67349	21.03	76.02	43.02	7.60	Fittings	25.40		
6/2/83		97.05						53349	76.02
		21.03							
(1)	(2)	(3)	(4)	(5)	(6)	(7)	(8)	(9)	(10)

You'll recognize the layout as being much the same as that in the cash book. Each row is for one invoice.

Column 1 The delivery date of goods received, or the date a cheque was sent.
Column 2 *Their* invoice number.
Column 3 The total amount owing to Abbott before this invoice was entered. (There is £21.03 under dispute on this account, so £21.03 is carried forward.)
Column 4 The invoice total including VAT.
Column 5 The amount of the invoice which refers to raw materials.

Column 6 The invoice VAT amount.

Column 7 As in the cash book, the name of the general ledger account to be charged apart from stock and VAT. In this case, there is £25.40 of fittings (shelves).

Column 8 The amount referred to in column 7.

Column 9 *Your* cheque number. The cheque will be made out a month after the invoice is recorded.

Column 10 The cheque amount. Record the date the cheque was sent.

Remember:

- Cheque writing and invoice recording are separate exercises
- Write 'P.L.' in the cheque book stub when you record a cheque on a supplier's card.

Throughout the month you just keep recording the invoices on their respective accounts. Invoices will come for January's deliveries well into February. Eventually, when nearly all the delivery notes have been matched to invoices, you can declare January closed. At this point you can get in some adding practice!

Month-end procedure The front card should be headed up *Control account.* You will be leaving the control card's 'General ledger account?' column blank, as you will the invoice number and cheque number. The date column will contain January. The other columns will be filled by adding up the entire entries for January from all the other cards. When you've finished, you can check your adding by checking that the control card columns add across in their own right. Remember, this is why its called a control account - you are controlling your adding. Whilst some accountants get a bit obsessed with checking their adding, it is certainly obvious that poor adding rather negates your record-keeping efforts.

We can now post this purchase ledger to the general ledger, using the control account card, as follows:

Total	to credit of creditors account
Stock	to debit of stock account
VAT	to debit of VAT account

Account £	to debit of overheads account (the details of which will be obtained by looking through the cards)
Cheque £	to debit of creditors account *and* to credit of bank account.

When the time comes for payment, it will of course involve one cheque for the balance (less any disputed items). *The cheque should only be signed if it is attached to the associated bundle of invoices and delivery notes.* Also, if the supplier has sent a statement of what *his* records show, this should be attached and reconciled to the monthly bundle (see Figure 4).

Sales ledger

You sell, on credit, to your debtors.

We can now move onto the sales ledger. *Here we are recording what is owed to you, so clarity and accuracy is of prime importance.*

If you are using a three-part invoice set, you will (1) get the customer to sign the set when he receives the goods, retaining his copy, (2) price up the two remaining copies, sending one to the customer in the post. Your copy will be used to enter up the sales ledger.

Again, because an alphabetical file seems logical, cards may be useful. They will not need to be so large this time.

Filling out cards Leave the first one for the sales ledger *control* card. Head the remaining cards as follows:

Account: BEST CUSTOMER LTD.

Tel: 051-239 4412
Address: 21 The House
M15 4PQ

Date	Invoice no.	VAT	Goods	Total (inc. VAT)	Cash	Discount	Outstanding balance
							21.43
4/1/83	4123	9.00	80.43	89.43			110.86
5/1/83	Cash				20.00		90.86
5/1/83	Discount					1.43	89.43

Figure 4 Purchase invoice routine.

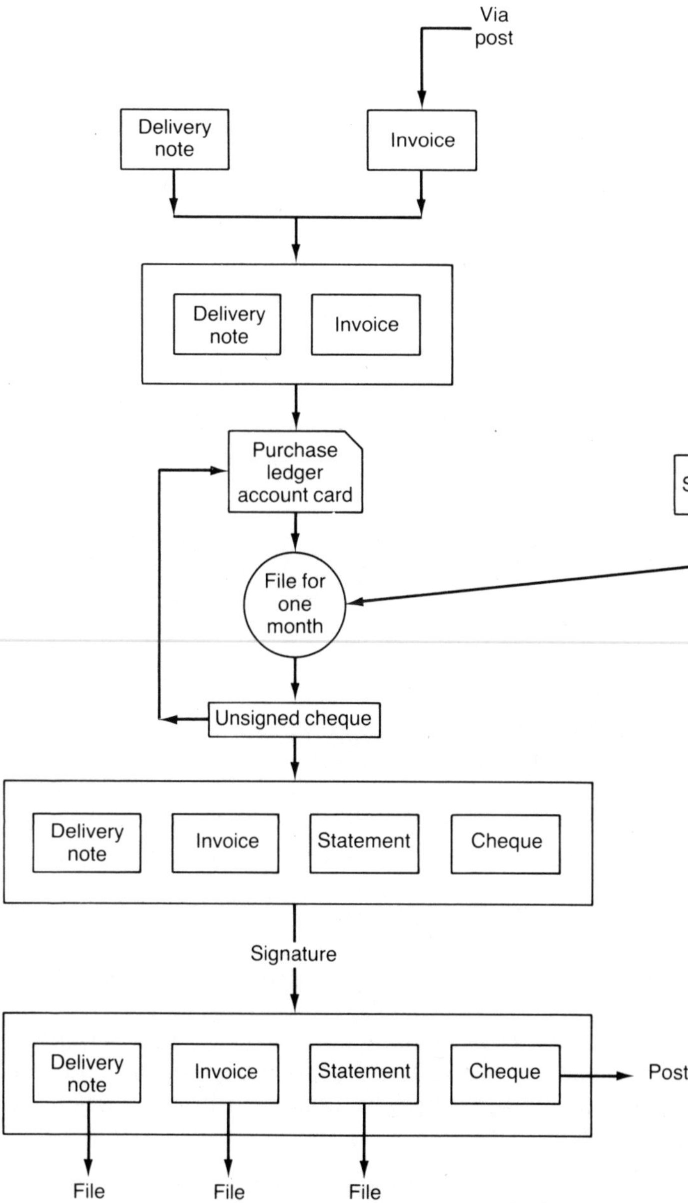

When your copy of the customer's invoice has been written up, it can be entered as above (invoice 4123). This customer owes you a total of £110.86 on 4th January 1983. It may not be due for payment yet if you allow one month's credit.

When the cash comes in, via the cash book, this can also be recorded as above. In this case £1.43 has been allowed as *settlement discount* (that is, because the customer paid promptly).

When giving (or taking) settlement discount you can work out an approximate annual interest rate by multiplying up the discount terms. That is, if the offer is 2% off if you pay one month early, then that is nearly the same as 24% per year. This 24% should be compared with your overdraft or deposit account rate before deciding whether to take up the offer.

Month-end procedure At the end of the month all the columns should be added up and totalled onto the sales ledger control account card (see Figure 5).

From the control card the postings to the general ledger will be as follows:

VAT	to credit of VAT account
Goods	to credit of sales account
Total	to debit of debtors account
Discount	to debit of discount-allowed account *and*
	to credit of debtors account

When writing or telephoning customers to remind them to pay, you could *photocopy their account card and send them that as a statement.*

Bank statement

We have nearly finshed our extra records system. The information we now wish to capture and analyse is the cheque book usage. So far (with the exception of changing our cash-in-hand level) we have ignored this important area.

The firm will write cheques for paying invoices, and for miscel-

Figure 5 Ledger controls.

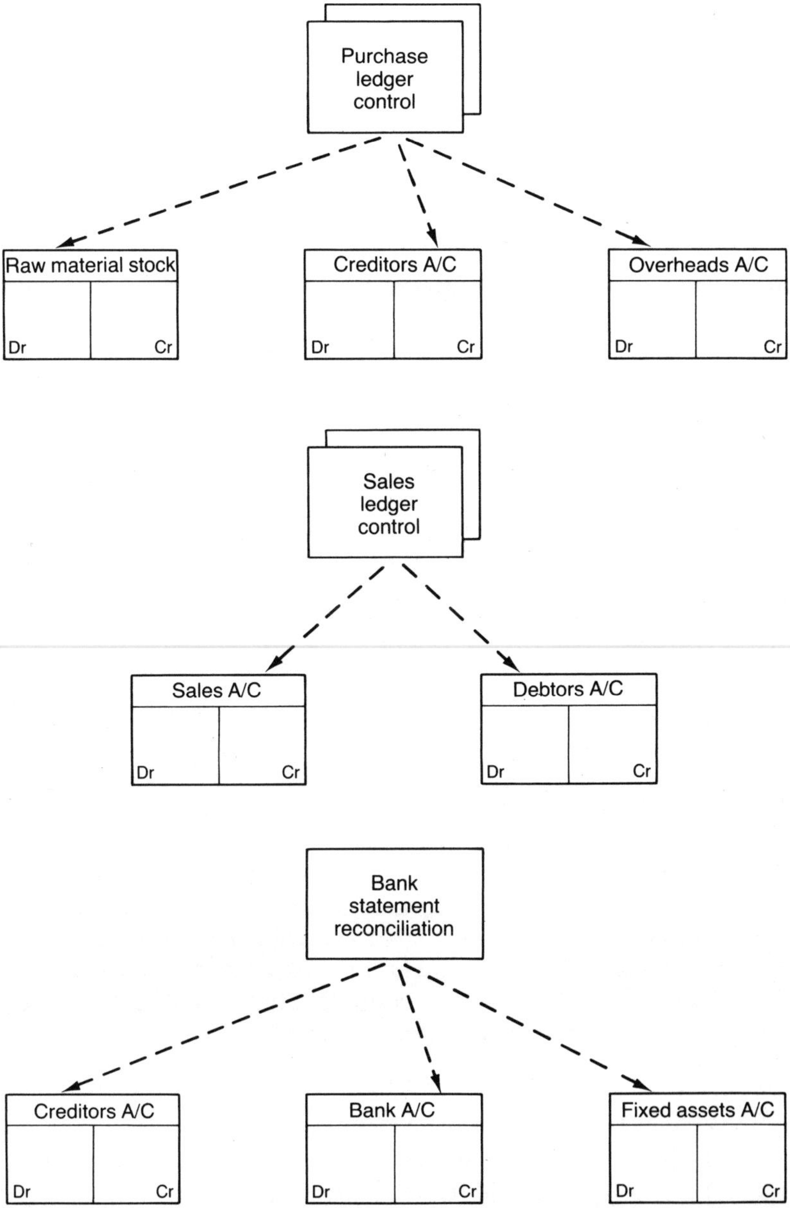

laneous items such as 'cash in advance' purchases. The vast majority of cheques will be those written out for the purchase ledger. *Full use of the purchase ledger should keep miscellaneous cheques to a minimum.*

Here we use the cheque stubs and the bank statement. First you should go through your stubs and check off your bank statement payments. Mark any cheques drawn for the cash book as 'cash book'. For any cheques not recorded in the purchase ledger, mark down the name (or number) of the appropriate account the cheque is to be charged to. For example, when you come to the cheque for VAT, write 'VAT account' next to the item.

Now get out the adding machine! Before you start to add, get a piece of plain paper and attach it to the front of the statements for the month, and lay it out as follows:

Bank Statement Analysis

(1) Purchase ledger	4507.36	Sales ledger	8014.88
(2) Cash book account	200.00	Cash book	921.12
(3) VAT account	1637.00	Others	0.00
(4) Loan repaid	1000.00		
(5) Interest charges	500.64		
	7845.00	Total	8936.00
		Opening balance	243.00
		Closing balance	1334.00

Posting: debit creditors £4507.36; credit bank £4507.36.

If the purchase ledger has been used as much as possible there should be few entries of the type listed in lines like (3), (4) and (5). (The actual entries in these lines will vary from firm to firm, of course.) These *special* items can now be posted. They will all be debit postings to the relevant accounts. The corresponding credit entry will be to the 'bank account', for example:

Debit VAT account	£1637.00
Credit bank account	£1637.00

Sales ledger and cash book totals do not have to be posted – they have already been entered in the cash book.

As your bank account should contain essentially the same information as your bank statement, you might try to reconcile them. *Your* balance will obviously be obtained by taking the difference between the debits and credits in the 'bank account' in the general ledger. When you try to reconcile them, remember (1) what you have yet to bank, and (2) that your outgoing cheques will take at least three days to get onto your bank statement. These cheques still going through the banking system are called 'unpresented' cheques. Good luck, it's often no easy task!

- A purchase ledger will tell you how much *you owe* to whom.
- A sales ledger will tell you how much *you are owed* by whom.
- A bank statement reconciliation will tell you how much *you owe* to the bank.
- Such information is essential for a firm's survival, because it is those to whom you owe money who can close your business down!

Action Guidelines

1 Check that *all* your customers and suppliers have a card account.

2 Look again at any 'miscellaneous' cheques you issued last month and ask yourself whether you are making proper use of the purchase ledger system.

3 On all invoices received, work out whether it is to your advantage to accept a discount for early payment (if offered!).

6

How to Close-off Your Books

- **The profit figure can only be approximate.**
- **The accuracy of the profit figure depends on the accuracy of the stocktaking.**
- **Monthly book-keeping is nowadays essential.**
- **The 'accumulated depreciation account'.**

You could just keep the cash book and purchase and sales ledgers, but more very useful information can now be easily calculated. This information is your profit!

Book-keeping may be an exact science, but what we are about to do is not. It is possible that after reading this unit you will never again believe in the sanctity of accountants or the word PROFIT.

Balancing-off

We are now going to prepare the general ledger prior to writing up the profit and loss account and the balance sheet. Before we work through the accounts, I must explain a routine known as 'balancing-off the accounts'. Let us assume that I open the general ledger and am faced with the following account:

Fixed assets: Cars account					17
Date	Item	£	Date	Item	£
	Purchase				
1/8/83	XTM 834R	3000.00			
24/8/83	TMH 149S	4000.00			
(1)	(2)	(3)	(4)	(5)	(6)

I would balance it off by first totalling the two '£' columns, i.e. columns (3) and (6). They come to £7000 and £0, but I put £7000 as a total on *both* sides. In order to make the data in column (6) add up to this total, I insert a line above of 'balance . . . £7000'. In good *double*-entry book-keeping style I must now post the debit entry to offset this credit entry (balance = £7000). The debit goes on the left – under the £7000 total, as follows:

Fixed assets: Cars account					17
Date	Item	£	Date	Item	£
1/8/83	XTM 834R	3000.00			
24/8/83	TMH 149S	4000.00		Balance	7000.00
		7000.00			7000.00
	Balance	7000.00			
(1)	(2)	(3)	(4)	(5)	(6)

The postings for the next month will begin after the left-hand side 'balance . . . £7000.00'. Next month's adding-up of the '£' column (3) and '£' column (6) will commence under the double lines.

So that is balancing-off, and is best done at each month-end prior to the preparation of a profit and loss account. When you have some proficiency at closing down the accounts, it may be possible for you to take a short-cut. Here the entry on the left-hand side ('balance . . . £7000.00') can be inserted in pencil. The totals £7000.00 elsewhere can be left off, as can all the lining-off. At the year-end, however, the auditor will want the accounts properly closed-off.

Month-end You can now balance-off all the accounts except the following:

Stocks
Cost of goods sold
Accruals
Prepayments
Overheads
Wages
Accumulated depreciation
Profit and loss account (this is not the profit reserve)
Sales

We shall now look at these a little more closely.

Stock account

You will remember that all the expenditure on materials was debited to the 'raw materials stock account'. This account will therefore now contain (1) an opening balance which represents the value of the opening stock, and (2) a month's purchases.

To obtain a closing balance (which represents the month-end raw materials stock) we just need to do a raw material stock count! If this does not suit you, then you will have to estimate the month-end stock value, and then confirm it whenever possible, say once every three months.

From this closing stock, which equals the new 'balance' figure in the debit side of the account, you can easily work back to the cost of raw materials used from stock:

	Raw material stock account					27	
	Date	Item	Debit £	Date	Item	Credit £	
revious month's ck-take	July 83	Balance	600.00	Aug. 83	To production	1250.00	by deduction
from rchase ger, etc.	Aug. 83	Purchases	1350.00	Aug. 83	Balance	700.00	from stock-take at month-end
			1950.00			1950.00	
	Aug. 83	Balance	700.00				

The 'To production £1250.00' posting is to an account usually called the 'work-in-progress account' (see Figure 6). This represents the production department. That is, we book raw materials (and later labour costs) into the account, and book out finished goods. If there is any work-in-progress at the end of the month this will represent unfinished items, and it has to be valued by a stock-take. Now, since we have (1) the opening balance, (2) the closing balance, and (3) the debit entry brought in from the raw material stock account, again - by subtracting the closing stock from the opening stock plus transfers in - we can make a *credit* entry in the work-in-progress account of 'To finished goods' (see Figure 6). The debit of this credit entry goes to the 'finished goods account'. Here again, a stock-take will provide the balance, and a credit posting will again be possible to show the goods sold. The debit to offset the finished goods account credit entry 'To sales (at cost value)' will be to a 'cost of goods sold account'. Here the run stops.

You need three stock figures, real or imaginary, to perform this run through:

- raw materials
- work-in-progress
- finished goods

The 'cost of goods sold (COGS) account' balance will be debited to the profit and loss account (P&L A/C). There it will be compared with the credit entry from the sales account, thus showing the 'gross profit'.

The costs included in the *cost* of goods sold includes (but only includes) *variable* production costs such as materials, piece-rate wages and other production expenses (for example, packaging). This means that the diagram is not exact, because the work-in-progress account will have piece-rate wage and packaging debited to it, as well as materials. By piece-rate wages we mean that part of the wages paid that *won't* be paid if nothing is produced. The other part of the wages of the operators, that is, the hourly rate, will be treated as a monthly cost (like electricity), and charged straight to the profit and loss account.

Figure 6 Closing-off accounts.

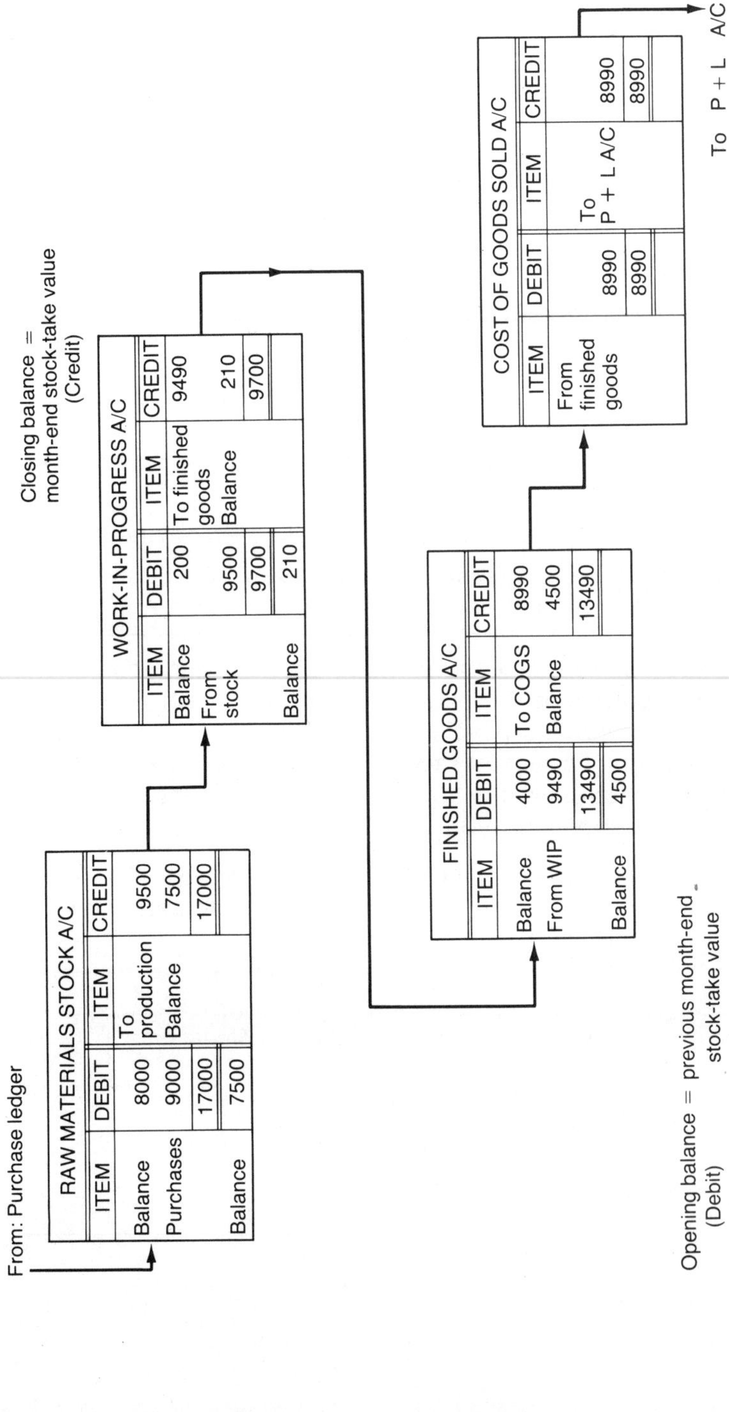

The closing of all these stock accounts will not be possible until the piece-rate wages and variable production costs have been posted into the work-in-progress account.

Overhead accounts

Exactly what overhead accounts you have decided to keep should reflect the type of business you are in.

As you go through each account the problem will arise of whether you have (1) paid for some overhead in advance, such as rates, or whether you have (2) used the service, but not yet recorded the bill, for example electricity.

- Bills not yet paid are called **Accruals**.
- Accruals are from **Creditors** (i.e. people to whom *you owe* money, e.g. electricity).
- Bills you have paid in advance are called **Prepayments**.
- Prepayments are to **Debtors** (i.e. people who will *owe you* money if you do not continue to use their service, e.g. rates).

Thus, you can turn up each account in turn asking yourself if the invoices recorded as debits on the account actually represent the cost of the overhead used so far this month. You can now see the advantage of a separate account for each overhead, that is, one for rent, one for rates, one for electricity, one for gas, etc. We shall show two examples for you.

Rates account In the account shown below you now want to close (balance-off) for the month-end prior to preparing the profit and loss account.

Rates account					27
Date	Item	Debit £	Date	Comments	Credit £
April 83	Purchase ledger	1200.00			

The entry for £1200 represents the *annual* rates bill you received from the council in April 1983. We shall assume that we are now closing for April 1983.

The annual rates bill is paid in advance. Thus, for April alone, the rates charge is one-twelth of this, which equals £100 per month. We wish to transfer an amount of £100 to the profit and loss account as our monthly cost of rates. So credit the rates account with £100, and debit the profit and loss account with the same amount. The remaining £1100 is a *prepayment.* We can thus clear this off to the prepayment account. So credit the rates account with £1100, and debit the prepayment account with £1100.

You will notice that we cannot have a balance left on any account that is not of a balance sheet item. Overheads, like cost of goods sold, and sales, do not appear on the balance sheet directly, so they cannot have balances left on them.

On our rates account we now have:

Rates account					27
Date	Item	Debit £	Date	Item	Credit £
April	Purchase	1200	April	To P&L	100
			April	To prepayments	1100
		1200			1200

Electricity account We shall still assume that we are closing April's accounts. In this case, say, we have used electricity during April, but have not yet received the bill from the electricity board. So when you open the account it will be completely blank.

You must estimate how much electricity you have used in April (you probably keep meter readings). Price up the units used at the rate per unit given on your last bill. Assume that you estimate you have used £85 of electricity in April. Thus £85 will appear in your April profit and loss account as an overhead (see below). You credit £85 to the electricity account and debit £85 to the profit and loss account. This £85 credit in the electricity account must be shown to have come from somewhere, and as you want *no* balances on overhead accounts, a debit entry somewhere of £85 is necessary – it's called an 'accrual'. The equal and opposite (credit) entry will be posted to the accrual account.

Thus your electricity account will look like:

Electricity account					21
Date	Item	Debit £	Date	Item	Credit £
April	Accrual	85.00	April	To P&L A/C	85.00
		85.00			85.00

Wages account

Before we consider the account it may be worth recalling the *logic* of the wage deductions. If you have no (contracted-out) pension scheme of your own, just ignore the figures for pensions.

With a tax code of 318H you are allowed to earn 318 × 10 = £3180 per year before you are due to pay any tax (the H simply means you are married). Your pension contribution is not liable to tax.

		£	
Pay (gross)		100.00	per week
Allowance (tax code)		61.15	i.e. £3180 ÷ 52 weeks
		38.85	
Pension per week		6.00	as company agreement
Amount due for tax		32.85	i.e. taxable part of pay
Tax at 30%		× 0.30	from Inland Revenue tables
Tax		9.85	
Gross pay	=	100.00	
Tax	=	9.85	
Pension	=	6.00	
Employee's NI	=	5.50	from tables, approx. 5½% of gross
Take-home pay		78.65	i.e. net pay

The cost of employing this person is £100 plus the employer's NI and pension contributions. The entries in the wage account should include all the employer's NI costs and pension costs.

You will need to identify how much of this wage cost was due to the piece-rate wages of the persons actually producing your product. Let us say that this is £60 of the total bill, which includes production workers' hourly rate and office staff, of £330. You want these £60 piece-rate wages in the work-in-progress account. What are the postings?

Out of wages account (credit £60) into WIP account (debit £60).

The difference, £270, can be sent to the profit and loss account as overhead wages. Thus credit the wages account with £270, debit the profit and loss account with £270. You have:

Wages account					19
Date	Item	Debit £	Date	Item	Credit £
April 83	Wages bill	330.00	April 83	To WIP	60.00
			April 83	To P&L A/C	270.00
		330.00			330.00

The 'wage deductions account' will show a credit balance, which means it is a creditor or liability to pay someone – the taxman. You will see it pop up in the balance sheet later.

Accumulated depreciation account

No doubt you have a good idea what depreciation is, especially if you are a car owner. It is the reduction in the value of an asset.

Original cost	= £5000	(two years ago)
Accumulated depreciation	= £2400	(over two years)
Present market value	= £2600	

In this example the firm has incurred a cost of £2400 over two years (£100 per month), for owning the car. This cost has to be charged to the profit and loss account. The original cost of the car is not charged to the profit and loss account, because it would rather distort the profit figure for the particular month in which you purchased the car. You would again distort the month's profit and loss account when you sold the car.

Thus, large costs for items that will last over some years are charged (debited) to an asset account, and only their depreciation charged to the profit and loss account each month.

There are three types of costs:

- those you can store (e.g. materials) and will charge to the profit and loss account as used;
- those you consume immediately (e.g. rent, rates, stationery, wages) and will charge to the profit and loss account on a monthly basis;
- those for large-cost long-term items (e.g. cars, buildings, machines) which are charged to the profit and loss account gradually, via their depreciation.

Some people call the first two *revenue* items, because they are usually purchased from sales revenue. The third are called *capital* items, because they are what you usually spend the company's initial capital on.

You have bought a car, and it now appears as a debit entry on your 'fixed assets - cars account'. The best way to determine by how much it has depreciated from the price you paid is to estimate the car's present market value. The difference (if it is now worth less) is properly called *accumulated depreciation.* The part of this total or accumulated depreciation that only refers to *this month* (April) is called the *monthly depreciation.* This means, of course, that the total of each month's monthly depreciation will equal the accumulated depreciation.

If you estimate the market value of your asset to be above what you paid for it, be prudent. I might be wise merely to assume it to be worth what you paid for it. Always remember you pay tax on profits!

What about some postings? You will need a 'monthly depreciation account' and an 'accumulated depreciation account'. If the *monthly* total of *all* your assets depreciation is £440, then the postings will be

Debit 'monthly depreciation' £440
Credit 'accumulated depreciation' £440

Each month the monthly depreciation will thus be added onto the accumulated figure. Next we want the monthly figure in the profit and loss account, so we

Credit 'monthly depreciation'
Debit 'profit and loss account'

Sales account

You will have a credit entry from your sales ledger postings. This merely has to be sent to the profit and loss account, that is:

Debit 'sales account'
Credit 'profit and loss account'

Costs come into the profit and loss account as debits, income comes into the profit and loss account as credits.

Accruals account

This account will now list all those costs incurred, but not yet billed for. This can simply be balanced-off, because it is a balance sheet item (you will find it on Arsenal's balance sheet in Unit 2). The reason we mention it here is that when you come to do next month's accounts the entries in this account must all be debited back out to their respective overhead accounts. This is because 'an amount for costs incurred but not billed for' can only be relevant to a certain period in time, the end of April say. For the end of May we must start again.

One of the first jobs when 'closing down' the accounts is to write back (cancel) the previous month's accruals (and prepayments).

Prepayments account

This is for costs we have been billed for, but not yet used. This again will have changed by the end of May, so all these debit items will have to be credited out then to their respective overhead accounts.

Work-in-progress account (revisited!)

You should now have (1) opening and closing balance (representing opening and closing stocks), (2) a debit for materials, (3) a debit for direct labour piece-rate wages, and (4) a debit entry for any other production expenses (these will come direct from the purchase ledger). You can now transfer the correct amount to the finished goods account (as mentioned before). This figure represents the basic cost of making the quantity of goods you produced during the month. The two sides will now have equal totals.

Finished goods account

Make both sides equal by posting the appropriate amount to the 'cost of goods sold' account (see before).

Cost of goods sold (COGS) account

Take the difference to the profit and loss account; that is:

Credit 'COGS account'
Debit 'profit and loss account'

You can *now* complete and examine your profit and loss account.

Figures 7 and 8 show in diagrammatic forms the principles we have been examining in this unit.

Figure 7 Stages in making up the monthly profit and loss account.

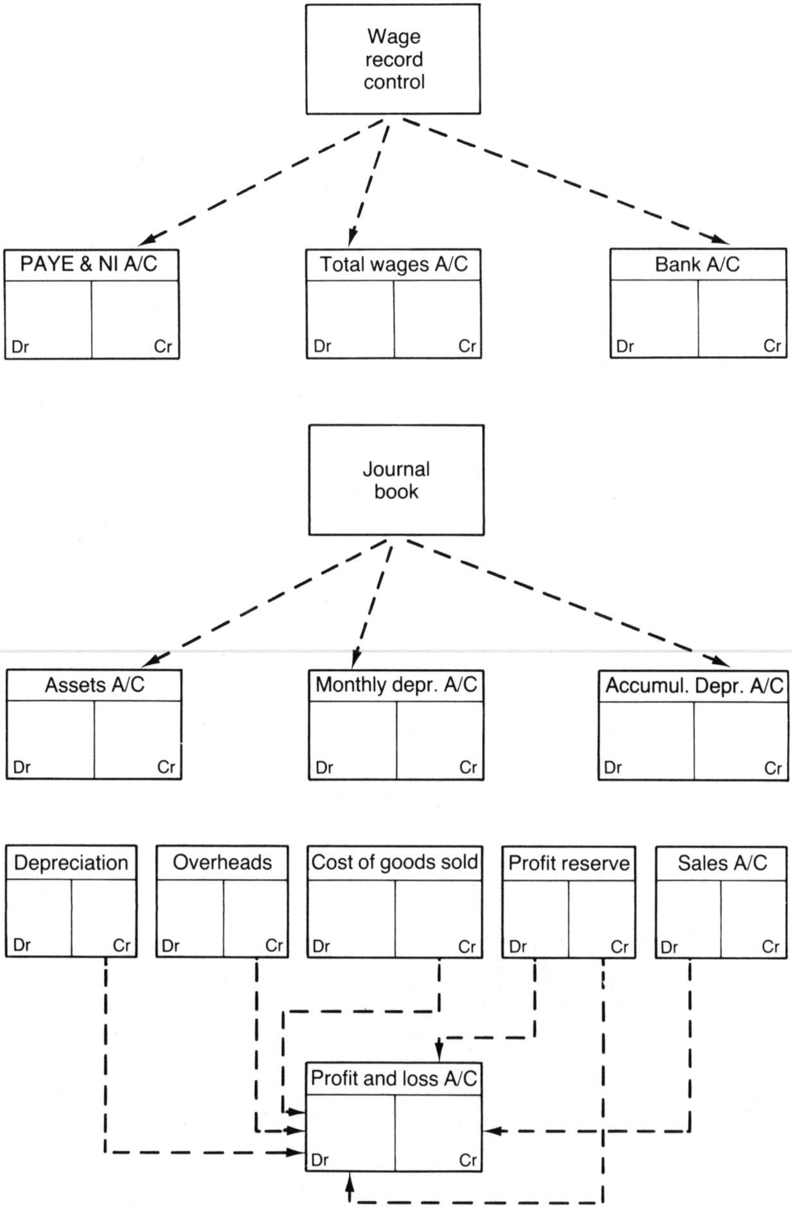

Figure 8 The complete picture. At the end of the month the balances are listed on the balance sheet.

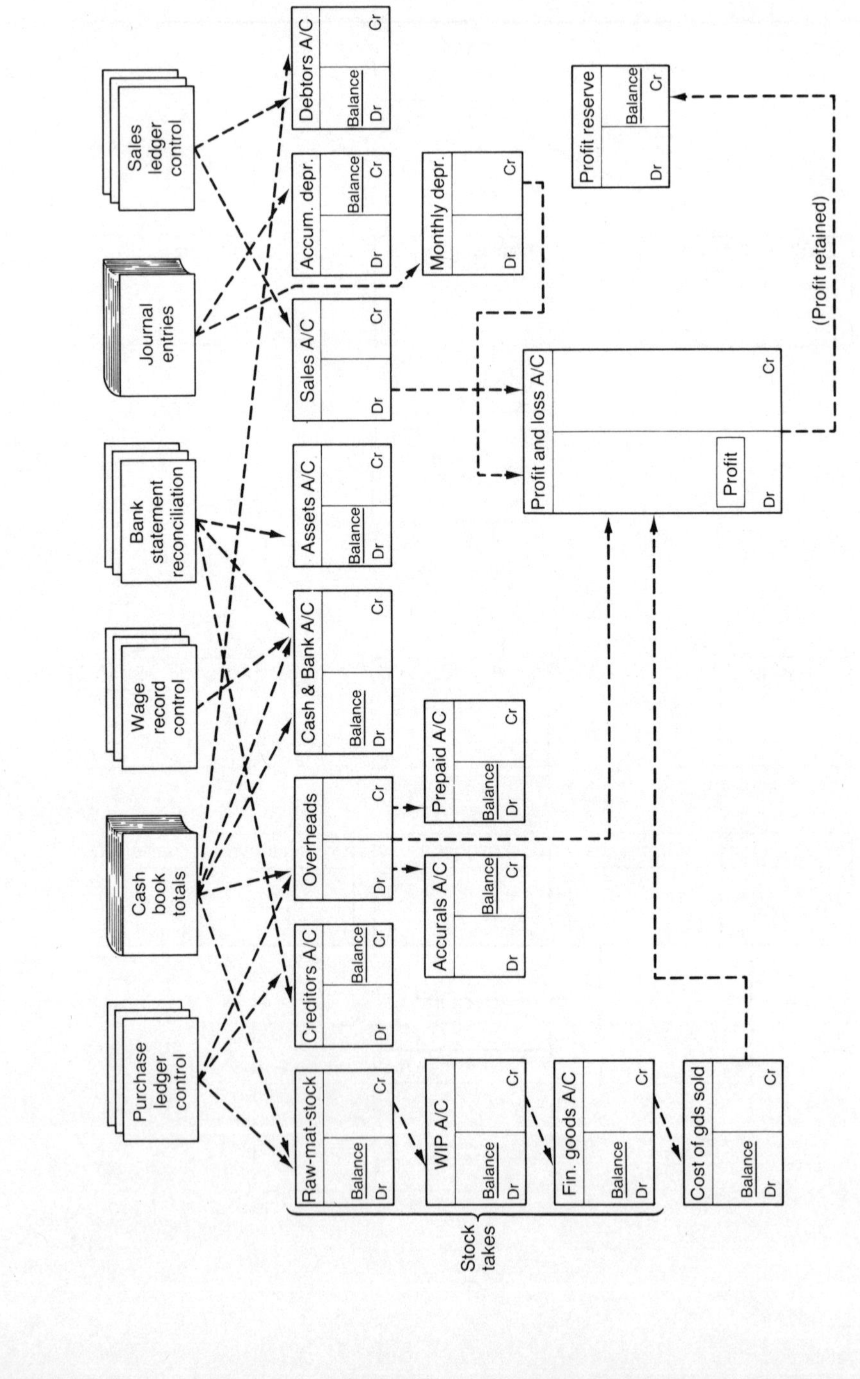

Action Guidelines

1. It is really worth your while to 'balance off' your books at the end of each month, without fail; there will be fewer nasty surprises, and you will always have your finger on the firm's pulse.

2. It is important to be familiar with the difference between revenue expenditure and capital expenditure. Make quite sure that you do recognize the difference each time you sign a cheque for anything. How, for example, would you deal in the accounts with a *substantial* purchase of stationery items?

3. When the accumulated depreciation of an item reaches the original amount paid, does that item cease to be an asset of the firm? Check that expensive items owned by your firm are being sensibly depreciated in the accounts each month.

7

Your Profit and Where Your Capital Is

- **Checking your profit and loss account to see how much your sales have cost you. The balance at the end is your profit.**
- **The balance sheet is just a list of all your month-end balances.**
- **The balance sheet shows how much money the firm is using, and how it is using it.**

The profit and loss account can now be examined a bit closer. You are in business to make a profit - here is how to calculate it.

You should now have an account in your general ledger that looks (after you have balanced it off) something like Table F.

It is a useful practice to balance-off this account before posting drawings (or dividends), then again afterwards.

What are balances (1) and (2)?

Balance (1) = month's *net profit* before tax and drawings (or dividends)
Balance (2) = month's *net profit retained* in the business (before tax).

Note the following:

- The tax is usually only deducted at year-end.
- The account is usually rewritten as a statement, much as Arsenal's profit and loss account (see later).

Table F
Profit and loss account 2

Date	Item	Debit £	Date	Item	Credit £
April 83	Cost of goods sold	8990.00	April 83	Sales	12050.00
,,	Advertising	141.00			
,,	Electricity	85.00			
,,	Cleaning	24.00			
,,	Depreciation	440.00			
,,	Discount	136.00			
,,	Rent	95.00			
,,	Rates	100.00			
,,	Office wages	270.00			
,,	Balance (1)	1769.00			
		12050.00			12050.00
,,	Drawings	700.00		Balance (1)	1769.00
,,	Balance (2)	1069.00			
		1769.00			1769.00
,,	To profit retained A/C	1069.00		Balance (2)	1069.00

- The discount on the sale's figure may be more meaningful as a negative item under the sale's figure.
- You might allocate a page per month just for the profit and loss account. These could be kept separate from the general ledger, if space demanded it.
- Balance (2) is posted to the 'profit reserves account' in the general ledger. Thus, a profit reserve balance will appear in the balance sheet.
- The legal requirement for limited companies to publish their profit and loss account only requires the firm to print details of sales (turnover), and from balance (1) downwards.
- If you want the *gross* profit, balance off after COGS.

So you have the month's profit. We hope it's a good one! Profit is only one measure of performance – there are many more, especially cash flow. Some consider profit a rather old-fashioned performance measure.

It is often interesting to see what percentage the profit is of the sales – that is, what overall net margin you made. It is usual to use *net* profit. Thus for our example

$$\frac{\text{net profit}}{\text{sales}} \times 100 = \frac{1769}{12050} \times 100 = 14.7\%$$

Balance sheet

We might now list all the balances left, in the general ledger. (Use the one below the double lines). This will serve two functions. First it will check your record keeping, especially for double entry. Second, and more important, you will be able to see in one statement what your liabilities are and how much you have invested in working capital this month-end. The balance sheet also serves, remember, as the basic document of accountability. It shows where your money has come from, and where (at the end of April) you have used it.

So your (list) balance sheet will look something like Table G.

A checklist

1 If the total of the debit balances and credits are not equal, your double-entry book-keeping has gone wrong.

2 This layout could be considerably improved both for the information it gives and for its visual impression.

3 If you subtract the accumulated depreciation from the fixed assets, you should get the 'written down' value of the assets. If the firm has just depreciated by reducing the initial cost to zero over, say, five years, then the net figure will be the 'net book value'.

4 Probably the most important figures here are the cash and bank figures. Most firms which cease trading have to do so because

Table G
List of Balances as at 30th April 1983

	(Debits) £	Credits £
Capital		50,000
Profit reserve		7,000
Creditors		10,000
VAT		500
Accruals		1,500
Wages liabilities		650
Bank overdraft		950
Fixed assets	50,950	
Accumulated depreciation		8,000
Stock (materials)	7,500	
,, (WIP)	210	
,, (finished goods)	4,500	
Debtors	14,890	
Prepayments	400	
Cash	150	
	78,600	78,600

they can no longer find enough cash to pay their immediate bills (ask Laker Airways).

5 The wages liabilities and creditors are usually added together.

6 It is often useful to show two consecutive months' balance sheets together for comparison.

7 The VAT account represents a debt due to the customs and excise people. There should be one account for each rate of VAT the firm pays (or receives). If this is impractical just have one account. This account can be used when completing the VAT quarterly returns.

The profit and loss account and the balance sheet have been rewritten in Tables H and I in neater forms. (The title 'working capital' used in the balance sheet means that part of the assets which is constantly changing from cash to goods, then back to cash.)

Table H Profit and loss account for April 1983		
	£	£
Gross sales	12,050	
Discount	(136)	
Net sales		11,914
Cost of goods sold		8,990
Gross profit		2,924
Overheads		
Advertising	141	
Electricity	85	
Cleaning	24	
Depreciation	440	
Rent	95	
Rates	100	
Office wages	270	1,155
Net profit		1,769
Drawings		700
Profit retained this month		1,069
Profit retained previously		5,931
Total retained (before tax)		7,000

Table I Balance sheet as at 30/4/83			
Net assets employed	£	£	£
Fixed assets		50,950	
Accumulated depreciation		8,000	
Written-down value			42,950
Current Assets			
Material stock	7,500		
WIP stock	210		
Finished goods stock	4,500		
Debtors	14,890		
Prepayments	400		
Cash	150		
		27,650	
Current Liabilities			
Creditors	10,650		
VAT	500		
Accruals	1,500		
Overdraft	950		
		13,600	
Working Capital			14,050
			57,000
Financed by			
Original capital		50,000	
Profit retained		7,000	
			57,000

Action Guidelines

1 You are in business to make a profit and you should now know how to calculate that important figure. Not being able to calculate your profit is rather like a lemonade manufacturer not being able to make lemonade! Calculate your last month's profit.

2. What do you think your bank manager will be looking for when he next sees your final accounts?

8

Have You Done Well?

- **Banks use ratio analysis prior to granting a loan.**
- **A profit of £20,000 is very satisfactory for a capital of £50,000, but it is poor for a capital of £200,000.**
- **If the bank immediately recalled half your overdraft, how would you fare?**
- **Are you seen as a good payer?**

Why analyse your accounts?

So you can now compile a profit and loss account and balance sheet, and have a good idea where the figures come from.

Can you, however, answer questions like:

- Can the firm repay its debts (such as an immediate call back of its overdraft)?
- If I purchased this firm, what return would I get on my investment?
- How much profit does it make on each £1 of sales?
- Are its stock and debtors at a *reasonable* level?
- How much capital does the firm need to return £1 of sales?

Such questions can only be answered by first calculating one item as a percentage of another (for example, profit to sales). This use of percentages to analyse a firm is called *ratio analysis*, and very revealing it can be.

Ratio analysis can be used to appraise your own firm, to appraise a competitor, or to appraise a firm you are interested in buying.

In order to demonstrate how to calculate typical ratios, we shall make use of the following three companies: PIE COMPANY, PEAS COMPANY and CHIPS COMPANY. Their profit and loss accounts and balance sheets are shown in Tables J and K.

Table J
Profit and loss accounts

	Pie company		*Peas company*		*Chips company*	
	£	£	£	£	£	£
Sales per year		50,000		30,000		20,000
Cost of sales		20,000		20,000		5,000
Gross profit		30,000		10,000		15,000
Selling expenses	5,000		2,000		6,000	
Office expenses	5,000		4,000		5,000	
Interest on loans	1,000		nil		2,000	
Total expenses		11,000		8,000		13,000
Net Profit		19,000		2,000		2,000

Materials are 80% of the cost of sales.

Goodwill is an amount that the present owner paid for a firm, over and above the purely market value of the individual assets. Thus, it is the extra price of buying a 'going concern' with all its customers, rather than just the buying of a 'heap' of assets.

Our analysis

Let us start with the ratio we have already done.

Question 1: 'What return will I get if I invest my money in buying this firm, assuming that I don't have to pay any more goodwill?'

Remember, return on capital invested equals profit divided by capital, multiplied by 100.

Table K
Balance sheets

	Pies company		Peas company		Chips company	
	£	£	£	£	£	£
Buildings	20,000		nil (rented)		10,000	
Machinery	15,000		5,000		10,000	
Furniture	5,000		1,000		5,000	
Fixed Assets		40,000		6,000		25,000
Stocks (finished goods)	5,000		6,000		1,000	
Trade debtors	5,000		1,500		4,000	
Cash	500		1,500		nil	
Current Assets		10,500		9,000		5,000
Trade creditors	(2,500)		(2,000)		(500)	
Taxation due	(8,000)		(1,000)		(1,000)	
Bank overdraft	(2,000)		(nil)		(2,000)	
Current Liabilities		(12,500)		(3,000)		(3,500)
Goodwill		7,500		nil		8,500
TOTAL NET ASSETS		45,000		12,000		35,000
Financed by:						
Initial capital	29,000		11,000		19,000	
Profit retained	11,000		1,000		1,000	
Total Proprietor's funds		40,000		12,000		20,000
Long-term loans		5,000		nil		15,000
TOTAL CAPITAL		45,000		12,000		35,000

	Pie Co.	*Peas Co.*	*Chips Co.*
Cost of firm (capital)	£40,000	£12,000	£20,000
Return (profit)	£19,000	£2,000	£2,000
ROCE	$\frac{19,000}{40,000} \times 100$	$\frac{2,000}{12,000} \times 100$	$\frac{2,000}{20,000} \times 100$
	= 47.5%	= 16.6%	= 10.0%

Clearly *Pie* Company gives the best return.

Question 2: 'What return will the present owner be getting on his initial capital?'

	Pie Co.	*Peas Co.*	*Chips Co.*
Capital	£29,000	£11,000	£19,000
Return	£19,000	£2,000	£2,000
Return on initial capital	$\frac{19,000}{29,000} \times 100$	$\frac{2,000}{11,000} \times 100$	$\frac{2,000}{19,000} \times 100$
	= 65.5%	= 18.2%	= 10.5%

The present owner has the advantage of having purchased some assets with retained profits.

Question 3: 'What *net* profit does the firm make per £1 sales?'

	Pie Co.	*Peas Co.*	*Chips Co.*
Net profit	£19,000	£2,000	£2,000
Sales	£50,000	£30,000	£20,000
Net profit per £1 of sales	$\frac{19,000}{50,000} \times £1$	$\frac{2,000}{30,000} \times £1$	$\frac{2,000}{20,000} \times £1$
	= 38 pence	= 6.6 pence	= 10 pence

Again, *Pie* Company seems the winner. The *gross* profit (sales - cost of sales) per £1 of sales are 60p, 33p and 75p.

Question 4: 'Which company spends the least on overheads, considering the level of sales it has?'

	Pie Co.	*Peas Co.*	*Chips Co.*
Overheads	£11,000	£8,000	£13,000
Sales	£50,000	£30,000	£20,000
Overheads per £1 of sales	22p	26p	65p

The Chips Company problem now becomes clear!

Question 5: 'Will any of the firms have problems repaying their interest payments?'

	Pie Co.	*Peas Co.*	*Chips Co.*
Interest	£1,000	nil	£2,000
Profit before interest	£20,000		£4,000
Number of times the profit exceeds the interest payments	20 times	N/A	2 times

Chips Company still has problems because the banks do not like to loan money unless the profit exceeds the interest at least *five times.*

Question 6: 'If the bank suddenly demanded its overdraft to be repaid, how would it affect the firm?'

	Pie Co.	*Peas Co.*	*Chips Co.*
Overdraft, less cash	£1,500	nil	£2,000
Current assets, less cash	£10,000		£5,000
% reduction in current assets needed to repay banks	15%		40%

Chips Company and Pie Company could repay their overdrafts without having to sell any fixed assets. Thus the firms could continue trading undamaged. However, while Pie Company would have to reduce its stock and debtors by 15 per cent only, Chips Company would need to reduce them by 40 per cent. Remember the bank wants its money immediately.

Question 7: 'If *all* the short-term creditors suddenly asked for their money immediately, how would the firms do?'

	Pie Co.	*Peas Co.*	*Chips Co.*
Current liabilities less cash	£12,000	£1,500	£3,500
Current assets, less cash	£10,000	£7,500	£5,000
% reduction in other current assets needed to repay liabilities	$\frac{12,000}{10,000} \times 100$ = 120%!	$\frac{1,500}{7,500} \times 100$ = 20%	$\frac{3,500}{5,000} \times 100$ = 70%

At last, a 'crack' in Pie Company's glossy image! A visual check on the balance would identify that if the tax man was due for payment soon the firm may be in trouble for cash.

Again, poor Chips Company has problems: an instant 70 per cent reduction in stock and debtors seems a hard task.

Question 8: 'How many week's stock is the firm holding?'

	Pie Co.	*Peas Co.*	*Chips Co.*
Stock (at cost)	£5,000	£6,000	£1,000
Cost of sales per year	£20,000	£20,000	£5,000
Weeks of stock	$\frac{5,000}{20,000} \times 52$	$\frac{6,000}{20,000} \times 52$	$\frac{1,000}{5,000} \times 52$
	= 13	= 15.6	= 10.4

What the correct number of weeks is for such firms cannot be guessed without some knowledge of their types of businesses. Peas Company looks high relative to the others.

In such a situation it may be more useful to know if the 'weeks of stock' is changing much over the years (or months). That is, the *trend* over a period of time of the stock may at least tell us if things are getting better or worse.

Question 9: 'How many weeks are debtors taking to pay, and how long is the firm taking to pay creditors on average?'

	Pie Co.	*Peas Co.*	*Chips Co.*
Debtors	£5,000	£1,500	£4,000
Sales	£50,000	£30,000	£20,000
Debtor weeks	5.2	2.6	10.4
Creditors	£2,500	£2,000	£500
Purchases	0.80 × 20,000	0.80 × 20,000	0.80 × 5,000
Creditor weeks	8.1	6.5	6.5

Chips Company comes up worst again! It allows its debtors the longest time to pay up, 10.4 weeks, but only takes (on average) 6.5 weeks to pay its bills.

Letting people take extended credit is like loaning them money. While *they* are not paying, *you* are paying interest on your overdraft, or foregoing interest by not investing it.

There is a tale about the successful grocer, who convinced a wholesaler to give him one month's credit terms. The small grocer then rushed off and sold his barrow-load of groceries, for cash, in two days. He then went back and purchased another load, larger this time, because of the profit on the first barrow-load. This growth continued in its rapid rate and within a matter of years the man had several shops. He had founded his business on the wholesaler's loans.

Question 10: 'How much of the firm's capital is invested in depreciating assets, as opposed to trading items like stock and debtors?'

	Pie Co.	*Peas Co.*	*Chips Co.*
Current assets minus current liabilities	£(2,000)	£6,000	£1,500
Total assets (less goodwill	£37,500	£12,000	£26,500
% working capital to fixed assets	0%	50%	5.7%

Pie Company and Chips Company seem to be heavily invested in depreciating assets, while the Peas Company seems to get by without being so. Again, the trend of this percentage may help us identify if Pie Company or Chips Company is slowly becoming a 'magpie' company (i.e. a horder of cash!).

Action Guidelines

1. We have looked 'between the lines' and learned some useful facts about three imaginary companies. Now do the same for your own firm. Only do the ratios that are useful to your situation.

2. If you wish, create your own new ratios.

3. Obtain a set of published accounts and analyse them. Obviously the best ones to have are those of your competitors(!), but if that is not possible choose a firm in a similar trade.

9

Value-Added Tax (VAT)

- **Does the VATman owe you money?**
- **VAT administration is just good book-keeping.**
- **VAT Form 1, VAT Form 100, or special schemes for retailers.**

For an in-depth appreciation of VAT you will need to consult the Customs and Excise booklets. Here I can help you with an overview and with some of the words used.

What is VAT?

It is a tax charged for increasing the cost (the value) of goods. When it was introduced, it was *hoped* that it would reduce costs and cut out middle-men. Some say it merely added to the rate of inflation by increasing costs, and therefore prices.

The person who *pays* the tax is the end consumer. For VAT purposes he is recognized as the person who is unregistered for VAT.

The persons who *administer* the VAT are companies who buy and sell goods or services.

There are two sections of VAT – the Input VAT and the Output VAT. the Input is the VAT your firm has to pay on its suppliers' invoices. The Output is the VAT your firm adds to its invoices. When you repay the Output VAT that you have collected for the VATman (Customs and Excise), you are allowed to *deduct* the VAT you had to pay on your purchases (Input VAT).

Your Input VAT (paid to your suppliers) includes all purchases for materials and overheads (e.g. petrol).

What are the VAT rates?
VAT is charged (usually) at four rates: standard, higher, zero and exempt.

- The standard rate is the normal one charged on most goods and services (now 15 per cent).
- The higher rate (if being used) is a larger rate charged on luxury goods.
- The zero rate means VAT is charged to the invoice at zero per cent (i.e. no VAT is added on).
- The exempt rate also means *no* VAT is added to the sales invoice. However, a person supplying goods exempt from Output VAT is unable to claim relief for the VAT he paid on his supplies.

A zero-rated company (that is, a company that sells goods which are zero-rated) would have a quarterly return to the VATman like this:

VAT paid	£2346
VAT received	0
due from VATman	£2346

An exempt firm will not get the £2346 rebate from the VATman.

There is no advantage (the opposite in fact) in not being registered for VAT, except a saving on the paperwork.

Your main problem then as the VATman's collector is to determine what rates of VAT to charge on various goods. For a merchant company this *could* include all four rates. For advice just telephone the local VATman.

How do I get started with VAT?

You need to register with the VATman. You do this by filling out a form. This form is called the VAT 1. After registration you will be asked to fill out another form every three months (i.e. quarterly). This form is called VAT 100. On this you summarize the details of the VAT you have paid out (Input VAT) and the VAT you have received (Output VAT). More of this later.

What paperwork is there?

The firm is required to maintain certain minimum accounting records. For most well-documented firms these are no burden. This is especially so if you keep the cash book and ledgers as we have suggested.

These records include tax invoices.

Your invoices should each carry clear details of:

- the date of the transaction (the tax point)
- the VAT rate charged (%).
- the VAT amount charged
- each invoice's unique number

These should be kept on file for at least three years.

The minimum records also include VAT accounts in your general ledger. You should (if the quantities involved warrant it) have a separate VAT account for each VAT rate. The *debit* entries in these accounts will represent the VAT you have paid on supplies (Input VAT); the credit entries will show the VAT you have paid on your sales. Provided you have made constructive use of the comments columns then this should keep the VATman happy.

You will make use of the VAT accounts by adding the debits for each quarter to calculate your Input Tax. This is then written into the quarterly return (form) VAT 100. You can add up the credits and insert this in the VAT 100 form as Output Tax.

Form VAT 1 (for registration)

We will now look in more detail at VAT 1. The form includes questions asking for this information:

- company name or owner's name
- trading style; the name used to trade under
- status of business - if private, limited, a partnership, etc. as recorded at Company House
- your registered address
- the address where most of your business is transacted, if different
- the address where the company accounts are kept, if different
- your business code (the VATman supplies numbers which classify your type of business for him)
- details of your sales (turnover) if you are registering but not legally obliged to do so. If you are keeping the necessary records anyway, voluntary registration seems sensible. The rules on who *has* to register changes from time to time. At the moment it is firms who sell more than £15,000 per year.
- an estimate of your *next* year's sales
- if you will be dealing in exempt goods. To answer this you will need the VATman to tell you what VAT rate applies to *your* goods. Exempt goods include education, health, betting, land
- if your Input tax is to be less than your Output tax. That is, are you likely to pay more VAT on your supplies than your sales. The reason for this question is so the VATman can know whether he can expect to repay you or if you will be repaying him (see example above)
- if your accounts are likely to be kept on a computer
- how you intend to pay (use a cheque)
- some bank account number
- why (if) you are applying voluntarily. Reasons include because you expect to grow soon or that you expect your payments of VAT to exceed your collection of VAT!

- why (if you are) you are asking for exemption from having to register. This applies to very few firms.
- your signature and date.
- any notices you would like to receive.

Form VAT 100

We shall now look at the form which you have to complete from your VAT account, every three months. Your cheque would normally accompany this return.

You will need to get a copy of VAT 100 in front of you to get full use of this section.

The form asks for your VAT number and the quarter (period) covered by the return. These are supplied by the VATman after registration.

Part A

Boxes (1)–(5) are for your total Output *VAT* collected for the VATman during this period. In box (2) you are asked to subdivide in parts and in boxes (3) and (4) for corrections from previous returns. Most small firms will only fill box (1) and repeat this as a total in box (5).

Boxes (6)–(9) are for the VAT you have paid on supplies (including overheads), i.e. Input VAT. Boxes (7) and (8) allow for errors from previous returns. For most small firms the total VAT paid will be in box (6) and repeated in box (9).

Box (10) allows for the calculated difference between the VAT paid (Input VAT) and VAT collected (Output VAT). Remember, if you have collected more than you have paid you will have to pay over the excess.

Part B

Here you record the goods value relative to the VAT amounts you have recorded in Part A (to the nearest £):

Goods	£100	(Part B)
15% VAT	£15	(Part A)
Total	£115	

The section is divided so that you can record the goods value corresponding to the different percentage rates charged.

Example

VAT rate	*Goods*	*VAT*	*Total*
15%	£1000	£150	£1150
	£500	0	£500
			£1650

This recording of the various goods value is required for both VAT collected and VAT paid.

Part C
If you are a retailer there are special schemes (see VAT publications) to save adminstration. In box (18) you enter the number of the scheme used. The obvious scheme is to allow retailers to trade with no invoices and assume all sales included VAT at one rate. The VAT can be calculated as a percentage of the total sales figure.

Part D
This concerns 'deductible Input tax'. Some of the VAT you have paid on supplies will be for personal use, for private cars and for entertaining British buyers. This VAT is *non-deductible* against your sales VAT. You should get your VATman to agree with you an acceptable way of separating these special items from your Input VAT. You might decide to total the amounts of VAT paid on these specials from the invoices themselves, if there are not too many of them. You might merely not separate the VAT on the invoice when recorded in the cash book or purchase ledger.

If you *sell* exempt goods you will only be allowed a reduced percentage of Input tax, i.e. less Input VAT will be deductible from your repayment of your Output VAT.

Part E. Your signature and the date.

The VATman will visit every so often to check the details on the form submitted by you, against your accounts.

Most firms will only have the VAT collected and tax-paid figures to enter on this universal form. Fill the form up to the best of your experience, and telephone the VATman with any enquiries.

Cash flow

VAT payments like any tax payments can be a sudden drain on the cash available in a firm. A good cash forecast will ensure the payment is not due at some inconvenient time.

Calculations

(When the VAT rate is 15%)

	£	
Goods	47.65	$\text{Goods} = \text{Total} \times \frac{100}{(100 + \text{VAT\%})} = £54.80 \times \frac{100}{115}$
VAT	7.15	$\text{VAT} = \text{Goods} \times \frac{\text{VAT\%}}{100} = \text{Total} \times \frac{\text{VAT\%}}{(100 + \text{VAT\%})} = £54.80 \times \frac{15}{115}$
Total	54.80	$\text{Total} = \text{Goods} + \left(\text{Goods} \times \frac{\text{VAT\%}}{100}\right)$

Action Guidelines

1 If you receive VAT rather than pay it, make sure you are claiming as soon as possible. VAT can cause cashflow problems.

2 Retailers should pay special attention to the schemes designed to help them - ask the VATman.

Section 2

Planning and Control

10

Costings

- **We now move from record keeping to forecasting.**
- **Costings are usually done on a per-unit or per-hour basis.**
- **You may have paid several different prices for a raw material, so you must decide which of these to use in your costings.**
- **Should costings assume good hard-working staff, or lazy slow ones?**
- **If you cost prior to working you then have a good control system.**

Why do costings?

If competitor's prices dictate the price you have to charge, costings will tell you how much profit you are making on each item.

On the other hand, if your product is so special that your customers will not be able to compare it with an alternative, costing will *help* you *determine* a selling price.

If you want to *control* the manufacture of your product, one method is to produce a detailed costing, assuming that an efficient worker does the job. This costing could then be used to compare the performances of other workers.

If you are trying to decide between two alternative methods of manufacture, costings for each method are essential.

Costings may have one of the following aims:

- to find the average cost per unit of a continuous repeated production process
- to find the exact cost of separately identifiable jobs which are repeated
- to find the exact cost of a very particular job which is most likely not going to be repeated

Rules of costing

We shall start with some general observations about costs.

Costs can be divided into those that vary as a result of the amount of production (*variable costs*), and those that vary as a result of the passage of time (*fixed costs*). Thus, during the firm's holidays or a strike the variable costs (e.g. materials) are saved. The fixed costs (e.g. rates, wages and interest) are not. At nil production, the total firm's costs will equal its fixed costs.

Try hard to avoid vague cost apportionments because they are usually meaningless. For example an apportionment like 'oh, shove on 20 per cent for overheads' is meaningless.

Do not charge the product with a cost until the product has actually received the charged work. For example, do not add the cost of packaging materials to an item that is in stock awaiting sale. This is important in stock valuations.

If you use up a cost (such as electricity), ensure that it is charged to the profit and loss account in the same month as it is used. For instance, do not charge electricity to a product (i.e. the WIP account) and then leave it in stock. If you did, this would stop the electricity charge from reaching the profit and loss account until the item was sold. If the sale was not for several months (even years), the debit in the P&L account, for electricity, would be held up for this time. You would be overstating your profit. We didn't charge electricity to the WIP account before, did we?

Production line costings

We shall now turn our attention to a costing system for a continuous production type company. This is the most straightforward to calculate.

Basically all we have to do is keep a record of the *variable* costs incurred in a month (e.g. sugar), and divide them by the quantity of goods produced.

The following calculation (which follows the same idea as the stock and WIP account calculations) will give us the quantity of sugar used in the month by a drinks manufacturer:

	lbs	at 15p/lb £
Opening stock	400	60
Purchases	1000	150
Available for use	1400	210
Less Closing stock	(500)	(75)
Used in production	900	135

This can be repeated for each material. The piece-rate wages for the month can be obtained from an analysis of the wages. The packaging costs can be calculated in the same way as for materials if the stock levels warrant it, or like wages if they don't.

The calculation of the quantity of finished goods produced can be done by (1) using counters on the production line, or (2) counting them into a finished goods store area, or (3) counting despatches to customers and doing a finished goods stock count. With this, the amount produced will be:

	Boxes
Quantity despatched	900
add Closing stock	90
Quantity available for despatch	990
less Opening stock	80
Number of boxes produced	910

Now we can simply list the month's usages (in £) and calculate the costs per unit, as shown in Table L.

Table L Unit (per box) costing 'Sunshine' drink			
	Month's cost (£) for 910 boxes	Pence/box	Pence/box
Sugar	60	6.59	
Glucose	15	1.65	
Flavouring	5	0.55	
Colouring	2	0.22	
Total materials	82		9.01
Piece-rate wages grade X	45	4.95	
,, ,, ,, Y	7	0.77	
			5.72
Packaging (labels)	2	0.22	
(bottles)	21	2.31	
			2.53
Total variable cost per box			17.26

There is an advantage in using the 'count the closing stock' method for materials, packaging, WIP and finished goods. It is that the cost of production includes such things as (1) loss via spillage or breakages, (2) loss via theft, and (3) loss via production methods.

So the cost to the firm of all these items is included in the final cost per unit. Remember, a loss, say due to a spillage, has the simple effect of increasing the cost per unit of that item.

If you have several uses for one raw material, you will also need to record how much is delivered to each use. If you have separate production stages you might have one WIP account for each.

You may decide to open a stock account on every material and a WIP account on every production stage. If you do, the total (or control) of all these accounts will be used like the stock and WIP accounts mentioned in an earlier unit. The size of your firm will determine if such record keeping is worth while.

Jobbing costing

Now we shall look at the costing method of a company that does various tasks to order. This type includes garage maintenance (e.g. services), servicing of machines, a small machine shop, a tailor, and even service companies like coach hire, despatch riders and even, if they wished, restaurants.

The first move with this type of costing is to identify what it is that controls the volume of throughput in your firm. We will call this 'thing' the 'limiting factor'. The limiting factor for a garage is usually the number of mechanics' hours available. For a forge, it may be the hours of forge time available. For a tailor, it may be the cutter's time *or* the sewing machine hours.

Of course these things can be changed, but let us consider the firm as it is. Let us assume here that the limiting factor for our firm is labour hours. We shall need to know:

- the total number of these hours available per *month*. That is, if we have 10 men working 40 hours per week, it would equal 1600 man hours, say
- the total of all the costs, except materials, per month
- the monthly profit (after drawings) hoped for.

Thus if the other costs (e.g. rent, rates, tools, machine depreciation and wages) come to £16,000 per month and the required profit is £2000, the charge per hour should be:

$$\frac{£16,000 + £2000}{1600 \text{ hours}} = £11.25 \text{ per hour}$$

So when a job comes in (1) the materials used on the job will be recorded on the invoice, and (2) the hours taken will be recorded. The two will later be priced up. The price of materials should be at cost - we already have our profit in the calculation. The hours in our case should be at £11.25. If details of this charge were shown to the customer, it would be shown as 'contribution to wages and overheads: £11.25 per hour for 20 hours = £225'.

It may be that the hours taken on a job would be stated as a standard time. Thus a six-foot gate may be recorded at the time the owner feels is appropriate and not the actual time taken. This would ensure that slow workmanship did not push up the rate for the job.

The way to improve on the *planned* profit is to:

- work faster than the standard time for a job
- work longer than 1600 hours, without changing the rate per hour
- charge more for materials than you paid
- save on wage rates and overheads used in the initial calculation.

Do not forget that if you don't work the basic 1600 hours, you'll not make the profit.

With this method of costing, the stock, WIP and finished goods accounts will be recorded mainly for purposes of recording *stocks.* It may be that there is no finished goods stock. Then work-in-progress would go straight to the cost of goods sold account (it may here be called 'cost of jobs done account'). There may also be no WIP account. If that is so, the materials used can go straight to the profit and loss account.

Unique jobs

If a job is completely new and unique the above method would still apply, except that:

- there could be no standard hours for the job
- the direct charges to the invoice may (with a large job) include items like special tools purchased for the job.

You will note that for these last two costing methods (i.e. for one-off items), the 'selling price' has been obtained. The objective of this unit was to talk about costs. The costs per hour can be found by deducting the profit from the overheads-plus-profit figure, and then dividing by the hours.

Your own situation

You will have to take these basic ideas and build you own firm's system around them. It is impossible to be too precise here because firms vary so much.

Note that we have avoided allocating overheads except where we have used the rate per hour. Remember that the telephone bill per unit is a meaningless figure!

Material costing

One problem we have been skipping over is how to cost materials. *Counting* them is easy enough; but for the cost figure should we use the cost when the materials were purchased, or the cost to replace the materials, or the cost of the last lot purchased, or some average of these? Our world of rising prices can make this into a problem. Add to this the problem of allowing for volume discounts, settlement discounts, delivery charges, rebates and container charges, and the problem looks unpleasant! Here are some thoughts on the matter:

1 The cost of materials must include the cost to get them to you.

2 Discounts for volume purchases are most easily handled as the cost of the material, not as an overhead reduction.

3 Settlement discount received (for paying on time or early) is usually entered as a separate overhead reduction.

4 Returnable containers are usually charged to an overhead account until returned. If large enough, a stock take may provide a balance which can be shown in the balance sheet. The balance sheet may have a sundries stock item for all small stock levels, not including production items. These sundry stocks may include machine spares, stationery and pallets, as well as returnable containers.

5 Rebates is a term usually used when a supplier allows you a reduction in price, if your annual purchases exceed a certain level. Thus a supplier may offer a 'rebate' of 1 per cent if total annual purchases exceed £5000, that is the rebate would be £50.

Which cost? What basic cost should be used on invoices when costs are constantly changing? There are a few choices possible, but by far the easiest to manage, and arguably the fairest, is the *last price paid.* It is easy because you just have to look up the last invoice. It is fair because it keeps up with inflation, that is, the method acknowledges that you have to replace the material, but does not make you guess the increased cost of the next delivery.

Such a method will not only be used on your invoices, but also when valuing your stock.

Action Guidelines

1 It is most important to ask yourself the right questions when doing a costing. These include:

(*a*) 'how many do I have to sell at this selling price to make a profit?' and

(*b*) 'why am I doing the costing?'
The answer to these questions, especially the last, will help you decide how to approach the costing itself.

2 Do not forget to include all relevant costs.

11

Pricing

- **Most firms have to compete for custom. Prices should be determined by what the market will bear.**
- **The price set will determine the volume that must be sold to make a reasonable profit.**
- **A graph can be drawn of price against volume for a chosen profit.**
- **Decide what is unique about your product or service.**
- **Beware of price wars.**

It is important to price your goods according to what the 'market place' is willing to pay. It is no use bragging of a large profit margin per item if you are not, in fact, selling many!

Sometimes it is difficult to know how many will sell at what price. Usually the higher the price the less sold, but there are notable exceptions. Dealers in antiques often claim that the way to clear items quickly is to put the prices up! A high price can give the image of quality in many brands of goods. The important thing, however, is that you *see your product as your customers see it.* Usually, that means it is just one of a choice that they have.

Supply and demand

To a person buying there are two main types of goods: (1) those which are plentiful in supply – with these the buyer merely chooses between various 'near-substitutes', and (2) those which are hard to get, or especially sought after – with these the price is secondary to supply. The second type can be thought of as unique.

We thus have a basic rule of the economist, that prices are set by the quantity supplied, and the demand for that supply.

The end result of this is that, unless you can convince your customers that your product is unique, your selling price will be strongly influenced by the prices that other suppliers are charging! This is true for most small firms.

Uniqueness

Some small businesses do offer a unique product. It may be that is what the business was founded on, for example, an invention.

Some small firms are founded on the idea that they can provide something which is established, at below the 'market' price. These firms should be careful not to forget their original ideas later.

If you want to charge above the market price you must attempt to convince potential customers of your uniqueness, which may be:

- speed
- convenience
- advisory service
- friendliness
- quality of workmanship

Remember to keep advertising this uniqueness to compensate for your higher prices.

Customer convenience or ignorance

So what, apart from uniqueness, can enable you to charge above the rate of a competitor ? One answer is *ignorance*.

In shops that sell a large range of different items, like wholesalers or retailers, the customers may be unable or unwilling to compare each price separately. Think of your local supermarket. You go there because (apart from convenience) you have noticed the price of *certain* items are below the price elsewhere. What about all the other items? You probably do not bother to check. You save yourself effort by assuming that the 'low-price' rule applies to all the other products on sale.

The shop owner must merely identify those products the customer will compare between shops. He can then charge market (or slightly below market) prices for those items. For the rest of his items he can, within reason, set his own prices.

For most firms pricing is the task of the salesmen, *not* the accountants.

Production line firms

How, specifically, would the owner of a firm supplying three non-unique items price his products? How would he then decide if it was worth his while being in business? Let us examine a simple example of a small soap manufacturer, whose figures look like this:

	Children's soap (£/bar)	*Men's soap* (£/bar)	*Ladies' soap* (£/bar)	
Materials	0.17	0.19	0.23	
Packaging	0.09	0.06	0.12	
Total	0.26	0.25	0.35	(from costing)
Selling price	0.43	0.31	0.48	(from customers)
Difference	0.17	0.06	0.13	

The correct term for the 'difference' above is 'the contribution' towards the *fixed* costs *and profits.*

The product recipe and purchase invoice costs will determine the material and packaging costs. The selling price will be supplied by observing what everybody else charges. To this market price that everybody else charges, one may be able to add a little for uniqueness (e.g. smell or wrapping).

After performing the above, you have the problem of deciding how many you should make *or* how many you can sell. The latter will *only* worry you if it is above your production capacity! One way around this problem is to ask, 'how many must I sell in order to make a profit?'

Assume that the firm's fixed costs come to £17,000. (Remember that these include all the remaining costs.) Next we must enter into a bit of trial-and-error guesswork.

QUESTION: Will you sell equal amounts of each type?
ANSWER: No, 50% of sales will be in ladies' soap
40% of sales will be in men's soap
10% of sales will be in children's soap.

QUESTION: Find N when £17,000 = (0.17 × N × 10%) + (0.06 × N × 40%) + (0.13 × N × 50%), and then apportion N, 10% to children, 40% to men and 50% to ladies. Alternatively, by trial-and-error find a quantity for each type of soap that will result in a £17,000 total when the unit contribution is multiplied by your quantity.

ANSWER:

	Children's	*Men's*	*Ladies'*	*Total*
Contribution	£0.17	£0.06	£0.13	—
Volume	16038	64151	80188	160378
	£2727	£3849	£10424	£17000

That is, you will have to sell:
16038 children's soap bars
64151 men's soap bars
80188 ladies' soap bars
just to break even, i.e. cover your costs, but make no profit.

QUESTION: Can you do it – can you make that many?
ANSWER: Slippery stuff soap!

QUESTION: How many bars of each will you have to make in order to show a net profit of £4000?
ANSWER: Do it yourself!

Jobbing firms, including service industries

We shall now look at the rather simpler case of firms that do jobs for which they are still only able to charge the 'going' (market) rate.

A costing here might look like:

Materials	£37.50
Labour, overheads and profit	
10 hours at £15/hr	£150.00
	£187.00

The £187.50 is the 'selling price', because the £15/hr included an allowance for profit. If every other firm is charging £12/hr, *or* if every other firm offers to do the job for £130.00, then there is a problem.

Here again we have to work backwards. You have to know whether you can do the job at these market prices. It is necessary to have *two* rates/hour figures available:

$$\frac{\text{Fixed costs plus desired profit}}{\text{Total man-hours available}} = \frac{£1200 + £600}{120 \text{ hours}} = £15/\text{hour}$$

$$\frac{\text{Fixed cost only}}{\text{Total man-hours}} = \frac{£1200}{120 \text{ hours}} = £10/\text{hour}$$

You can now use the £15 as WHAT YOU WOULD LIKE TO CHARGE, and the £10 as THE LEAST *YOU* CAN DO IT FOR.

So, going back to the £130 job: as you *can't* get £187.50 for the job, you want to do it for more than:

Materials	£37.50
Overheads	
10 hours at £10/hr	£100.00
	£137.50

This job would probably have to be turned down, but see later in this unit under **Minimum price**.

If you could go to £12 per hour the profit would be reduced to:

(£12 × 120) − 1200 = £240

Cost-plus for production line

It may be that you *are* in that very unusual and happy position of being able to dictate the selling price to your customers. 'Take it or leave it, there are plenty willing to pay that.'

On the other hand, it may be that you are not willing to make as many as you *could* sell, so you can 'pitch' the price high and thus reduce the numbers buying.

It may also be that you have not the time to, and do not see the need to, go around finding out what the market place is willing to pay. This might apply, remember, to a wholesaler or retailer.

If the above includes you, then the pricing system of 'cost-plus' can be used. You total your costs and just add a percentage (a mark-up) for yourself. For example:

	£/box	
Materials	0.43	
Piece-rate labour	0.10	
Packaging	0.05	
Total	0.58	(variable cost)
Mark-up 55%	0.32	
Selling price	0.90	

The mark-up of 55 per cent here (multiplied by the quantity sold) is to pay for your *fixed costs* as well as your *profit*. Suppose the fixed costs are £300 and the profit sought £212 (total £512). This £512 will be achieved when 1600 boxes have been sold (i.e. 1600 × £0.32 = £512).

Working out the mark-up percentage Work out what variable costs you will incur (that is, for materials, etc.). This step depends on a good sale's forecast or a statement from you as to how many you are willing to sell. Assume that you work the total variable costs out as £928. Then:

Total variable costs per box = £928

Fixed costs plus profit = £512

$$\text{Mark-up} = \frac{£512}{£928} \times 100 = 55\%$$

Remember that *mark-up* is a percentage of variable cost; *margin* is a percentage of sales volume.

For jobbing firms, independent of the competition, the rate per hour (including the desired profit) would be used rigidly.

Minimum price

Would you ever sell, or take on a job, when the price quoted did not even cover your fixed costs. That is, using the example from the jobbing firm earlier:

If hoped-for rate = £15/hour
If rate to only cover fixed costs (no profit) = £10/hour
Would you ever work for £8/hour?

We are clearly on dangerous ground here, because if you worked for £8/hour on all jobs you would not be able to pay for your fixed costs, and you would go out of business.

However, you might work at £8/hour on the occasional job if you thought the job could introduce you to better things, or if times were bad and there was no alternative.

The logic of working for £8/hour is that it at least earns you money *towards* your fixed costs. This must be better than earning nothing towards them. Remember, fixed costs are paid for by the minute. Every minute the firm exists, the fixed costs are adding up. The £8/hour is a 'contribution' towards your fixed costs.

Price wars

Before we leave this important subject area of prices a word about 'price wars'.

There are several factors which influence a customer into buying your product or service. Price is only one – others include convenience, quality, advice and packaging.

One of the easiest, most dangerous, of management actions is to start offering goods at prices *below* that of competitors. This is especially true if you are 'taking on' a large group of companies.

These groups can afford to sell your type of products at a loss *for a while*; can you?

You should only offer cheaper prices if your production methods genuinely can provide the item more cheaply. This does not usually include having less administration costs. Also remember to calculate the impact of another supplier (yourself) coming onto the scene. The number of customers will be spread over more suppliers.

Don't enter price wars unless your production method genuinely offers you some cost reduction.

Why cut your prices and thus your profit per unit? Why not compete in other ways, win the customers *and* maintain your profit per unit.

Volume

You will have noticed how important volumes were in all the above discussions about price setting. The more you sell the lower your sales price can be.

Also, we have been talking about the 'before the sale' situation. We shall now look at the month- (or year-) end situation.

The basic question here is, '*at what volume of sales will my firm start making a profit*?' This could be a useful figure to keep in your head just to enable you to stay on top of things.

Imagine that with sales at £18,000 your profit and loss account showed a profit of £3000. Further suppose that your fixed costs were £12,000. You could draw the chart shown in Figure 9.

If you follow the line OS (sales revenue) upwards, you will notice that it is below the total cost line (FC) until it reaches B. This part is called the *break-even point.*

The difference between the line FC (total costs) and the line OS (sales revenue) equals profit. Thus, when the level of activity (V) is below B the firm makes a loss, above it makes a gain. By activity we mean sales. B is measured as a level of sales called the 'break-even sales level'.

Figure 9 'At what volume of sales will I make a profit?'
OF = fixed costs of £12,000
OR = sales revenue of £18,000
OV = the volume of activity, in this case £18,000 sales
VC = total costs for £18,000 sales = £15,000
SC = profit

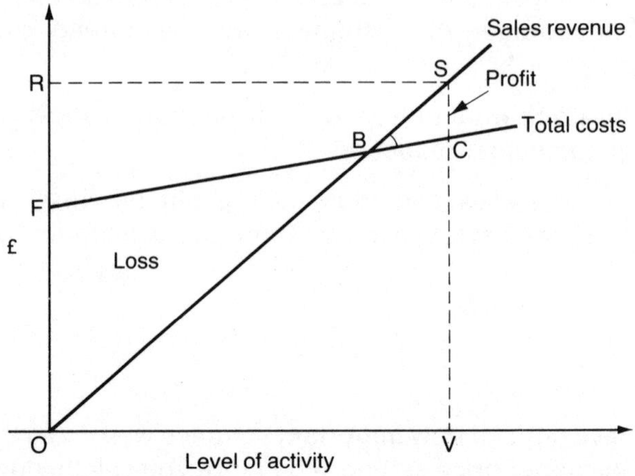

Drawing the chart Whilst here we have drawn the total-cost line and the sales-revenue line by just knowing points F, S and C, this is a bit naive. If you draw one of these break-even charts you should plot various values of S for different levels of sales. Then, remembering that at zero sales there is zero revenue, draw a 'fair' line through all your plots.

Next plot the various values of C for different levels of sales, and then draw the fairest line through the middle of them. Extend this line back to the vertical axis and thus find F.

If your business is seasonal, or liable to fluctuation, you should be able to obtain the necessary sales and cost figures from the profit and loss account.

Use of the chart So what do you learn from the chart?

1 It will tell you the level of sales you need to earn a profit. You must be past point B. You could convert this to a daily sales figure, or to some other convenient measure such as hours worked per day. You would then have a rough guide to your performance each day. Knowing you need to work, say, 40 hours per day to break even, and you'd worked 50 hours, you would know that that day you had made a profit.

2 The wider the angle SBC, the larger the margin you are making per £1 of sales.

3 It can make a useful chart to use to keep employees abreast of the firm's performance. You may explain where the profit is spent - that is, in tax, reinvestment and the owner's drawings.

Be warned that one chart represents one firm, for a certain mix of sales items, and for costs at a certain level. These factors change, so the chart goes out of date. You will need to renew it.

A variant There is a variant of the chart which enables you to read profit off directly. It is shown in Figure 10. Marked on it is the profit for £18,000 of sales. You can draw this from your profit and loss account.

Figure 10 Profit against sales revenue.

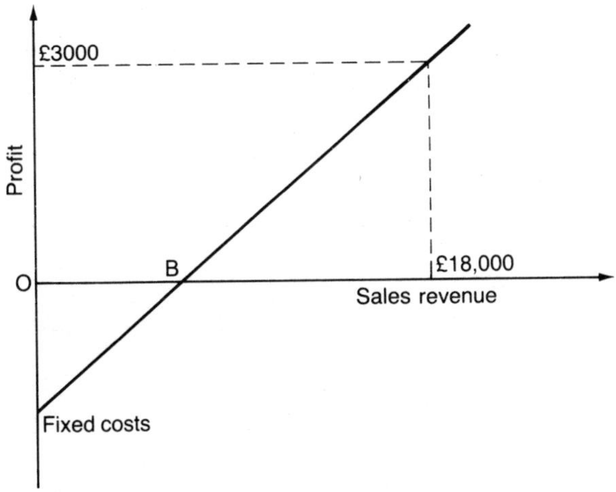

Action Guidelines

1 Have you decided what is unique about your product or service? Even if you have never seen your business in this way before, force yourself to come up with an answer to this question. At the very least, thinking about it will give you a valuable insight into your business and what you are trying to do.

2 Be clear in your mind which type of business you are running. Is it one for which you have comparative freedom to set your prices?

3 Think whether you can add something to your service or product without greatly increasing the fixed or variable costs, so that you have more scope for claiming a 'uniqueness' in what you are offering.

12

Control Your Costs

- **Cost savings follow from careful managerial judgement.**
- **Time is money.**
- **Good planning reduces costs.**
- **Materials stocks must be managed.**
- **Should you be insured?**

Saving costs can be a double-edged sword. On the one hand you reduce your costs, on the other you might reduce your sales.

'Saving' money by not using the telephone may mean missed orders, missed information or a debt repayment delay. It may, on the other hand, merely mean a smaller bill!

'Saving' money by buying cheap materials can lead to increased labour costs, increased wastage or inferior finished goods. On the other hand, think twice before using stainless steel when plastic would do!

Thus we are caught somewhere between two extremes, and a compromise, a managerial judgement, must be made. That is *your* problem and one of the things that separates good managers from bad. If you feel you are *always* finding this optimum cost, you most likely are not. It is a complex and continuous task, well worthy of your clearest thoughts and best attention.

Materials

Sometimes it is difficult to tell the difference between fraud, mistakes and carelessness. We shall therefore not separate them, but just look at your control over your materials.

You must check that you are getting exactly what you have ordered and paid for. Take time to check whilst the supplier is still present. Do not sign or pay until you have checked - this can save hours later.

Measure and value all your *wastage*. Wastage comes from deterioration in stores, damage, and normal production processes. Unless you keep a check on this it can grow alarmingly. A firm's waste will tell you a lot about a firm's management. You should also not be too quick to dismiss waste as valueless. Remember, metals are recycled, unwanted food can go to pigs, chemicals be used as fertilizer.

There is the tale of a small businessman who used to be *paid* for taking away the ash from his local power-station. He then bagged it and sold it! His profit and loss account would be a sight for sore eyes.

Check that your storekeeping is efficient. This area can be a source of a lot of financial waste. Remember the objectives of good storekeeping include

- easy *access* to materials
- immediate *location* of materials (how often do you reorder, just to find some more hidden away?)
- full and easy *identification* of the material, so you know what you have got in your hand
- economical use of storage space (but at the same time remembering access, etc.)
- adequate but not excessive protection against fire and theft
- adequate protection against deterioration from water, heat, damage
- having a good rotation system
- comparative ease for counting

Overstocking and understocking The other side of storekeeping is to ensure you do not overstock or understock. Overstocking leads to wasted money tied up in an *overdraft,* in space (that is, rent and rates), in insurance costs, and in equipment costs (bins, pallets, etc.). There is also the risk of obsolescence and deterioration. It does, however, save the time of continual reordering!

Understocking can lead to lost orders (and therefore reputation) and disrupted production and wasted set-up times.

The proof of good materials management is in how much time you spend arguing with suppliers, returning goods, and how much money you throw away in scrap.

Stock count You *must* be roughly aware of how *much* stock you have at any point in time. Stock includes raw materials, work-in-progress and finished goods.

How often you actually go around and count the stock will depend on how much stock your type of business has to carry. Once a year will be the minimum (for your year-end audited accounts). Daily stock takes *may* be necessary for some retailers.

The more often you count your stock, the more control you have over it. You will of course have to set this knowledge against the cost of the time taken in counting.

Some firms adopt what is called 'continuous stock-taking'. One day they count one item or type, and the next day they count another item.

The stock count is important since an overstatement of the quantity of year-end stock will result in an overstatement of that year's profit. This fact leads some accountants to prefer the stockcount to be made by someone who will not benefit from the stated annual profit. However, some owners say that they must count their own stock as a control over fraud and bad stores management.

Management of the workforce

We shall now take a general look at the management of labour. We shall be talking about an expensive, emotional, contracted material.

It used to be a north-country saying that the only quality a man need look for in a wife was her willingness and ability to work hard. Having this, happiness and wealth would follow! This principle must be true of a workforce, but life is not as simple as proverbs.

> Your workforce should be:
>
> - intelligent, and given an adequate chance to use this intelligence
> - motivated with job satisfaction and pride in addition to fair remuneration
> - well led, without ranting and raving from the management.

Interviews These are crucial. A lot of money can be saved if you can avoid recruiting people who leave just after you have expensively trained them. The employment of someone who does not get on well with existing personnel can cause you problems.

Give interviews your best attention. Plan them properly. Do not just rely on government agencies – go out and look for someone. If you want a pretty counter girl, go around the shops looking for one! Advertisements in newspapers *tend* to attract the short-stay types.

When candidates come to you make sure you know what you are being offered. Can a twenty minute chat be enough for you to make an investment of say £5000 a year, for many years?

In a small business your biggest assets may well be your staff (no matter what the balance sheet says!). Think well before you spend.

Idle time Labour costs are consumed with every tick of the clock – you can't store them. This means that a manager's biggest enemy is idle time. Do not impose unreasonable workloads, but do not keep staff waiting around for a machine or a toilet. The only answer to this is good work scheduling. A queue at work is an insult to the boss!

Salaries

This is usually one of the largest overheads. Remember the cost of employing someone includes:

- their salary
- the employer's NI contribution
- tax and NI administration
- desk and chair
- toilet facilities
- refreshment facilities
- heat, light and power
- possibly a telephone extension
- training

The good use of part-time workers often increases the availability of labour and the output per hour.

Other overheads

Rent Over a long period this can be expensive compared with the cost of owning, especially if you take account of the way buildings have been increasing in value. Your location can be crucial to a small business, so make sure you do not locate yourself badly just to save a little rent.

Ensure that you have a formal rental agreement, and a good record of rent payments. Pay by cheque. Consider the sub-letting allowed, or not, in your rental agreement.

Make use of 'enterprise zones' where possible. These are special low-rent low-rates planning-permission-free areas set up by the local government. Ask at the Town Hall.

Ensure that the premises satisfy the Health and Safety Acts with regard to toilets, painting, and space per employee.

Many small firms make good use of unwanted council properties.

Rates *Check the bill thoroughly* – the council is under no criminal liability to charge you correctly!

Again, consider enterprise zones or local 'special' areas (enquire at your Town Hall).

Avoid monthly payment schemes – they are designed to make you pay earlier, and therefore more. As with all bills, leave it until just before the deadline before paying.

Make sure you get the services you pay for. The general standard of roads, lights and buildings around you are important to your firm's image. Make sure the council is keeping them up to scratch, and bring deficiencies to its notice. Make sure you have police protection at night.

Power Consider the impact of strikes on your supply of gas, electricity, oil and coal.

Conduct tests on whether having a boiler on all the time is cheaper than switching it on and off. Use meters where possible, more than one if necessary.

Use indirect heat (that is radiators), rather than direct (open fires) where possible. Remember that heat rises, so do not let too much blow away up chimneys, and locate people *over* hot machines - that is, have machines downstairs, offices upstairs.

Thick materials for roofs and walls stops freezing in winter, frying in summer. Make maximum use of that free heat source, the sun. Look for south-facing premises, make maximum use of the daylight hours, stay away from exposed locations (hill tops), and place your buildings next to or on top of each other.

When it comes to paying the bills, remember to compare the *units* used (compared with the same month last year), rather than the costs. Do not pay these bills too early.

Repairs and maintenance This is something you should consider when you buy a piece of equipment. Make sure that you collect the guarantee when you buy something, and file it carefully. Remember, the Sale of Goods Act states that it is the *seller's* responsibility to sell reasonable goods, regardless of any guarantee.

If the piece of equipment is complex (a computer, a photocopier, an electronic machine), under some leasing agreements maintenance is included in the cost.

Be careful to get rid of equipment when it costs you too much to maintain. Keep records in your general ledger of *what* maintenance bills are for. In this way costly machines will soon show up.

Telephones and telex Local telephone calls are cheaper than stamps, provided you don't talk for more than three minutes. Never hang on for someone – ring back, or better still ask them to ring you.

Consider buying or renting an answering machine. They are convenient, but some callers are offended by them.

Employee's will *need* to make *some* personal calls – a *pay-phone* may help.

Telephones can save you time, if you 'let your fingers do the walking'. Before going anywhere check on the 'phone first.

Telex is cheaper than the telephone provided you use it correctly (that is, use the paper tape). It is a very good way of getting a letter to numerous persons. It is therefore especially useful in:

- chasing or reminding debtors to pay up
- confirming orders
- confirming verbal agreements
- overseas trade.

You can rent a telex or make use of someone else's.

Photocopier This can be both a blessing and a curse. It has great *potential* to save time and cost, but it often ends up as an unnecessary creator of paper. Therefore, make it inconvenient to use by

- locating it somewhere inconvenient or under your eye
- not getting a 'super' fast one
- making users record what they have used it for

Do not let it replace carbon copies. It can, however, save typing time by being used to photocopy a letter you have received, which, with your comments on it, is used as your reply.

It may be wise occasionally to withdraw it from service to see how 'hooked' people have become.

If possible, pay to use someone else's until your need is large enough to buy or lease your own.

Typing Customers will be impressed by good typing. That includes a nice print and a nice layout. Electric typewriters can provide nicely typed letters more quickly than can a manual machine.

Internal letters should *never* be typed. Furthermore, the use of felt pen messages which rub away with a cloth on plastic boards can replace typed notices. When replying to a letter, where possible, just write your comments on the bottom, changing 'Dear' to 'From'.

Professional fees Clear up the matter of cost *before* you use a professional person's services. Remember that they too are small businessmen sometimes ready to do deals. Insist on an itemized (detailed) bill.

You could make use of schemes arranged to avoid hiring professionals. These include:

- buying limited companies off-the-shelf, as advertised, for example, in accounting journals
- collecting your bad debts through the County Court Scheme
- doing your own accounts

Compare different advisers' fees. Advisers include solicitors, accountants and banks.

Confirm in writing (and keep a copy of) any instructions you give the adviser. *Do not* let him write to you – it will cost you!

Ensure that you are not paying for their delays. If you are selling a property and your solicitor threatens to take three weeks holiday, threaten to deduct the mortgage repayment for those three weeks from his bill!

Advertising People must be attracted to, and informed about, your products. It is rubbish to say 'a good product sells itself' – it doesn't.

Try to measure the impact of your advertisements on your customers. Ask them where they heard about you, and where they have come from. The head of Lever Brothers once said, 'With advertising at least fifty per cent of what you spend is wasted; the trouble is knowing which fifty per cent!'

Clearly identify the role, and users, of your product before advertising.

If you advertise be ready to receive enquiries. Stock up and make sure the telephone is manned.

See the companion book in this series, *How to Win Profitable Business.*

Insurance Types of insurance include:

- life assurance; on your, your partners' and key employees' lives
- pension assurance; for you, partners and employees
- marine; on ships and cargo
- aviation; on planes, passengers and cargo
- fire; lightning and explosions
- special perils; including riots, objects from the air, storm, tempest, flood, water (tanks, pipes), impact (lorries, horses, cars, etc.), spontaneous fermentation, heating or combustion (vegetables, coal, chemicals).
- profit; for lost profit owing, say, to a fire
- accident fidelity guarantee; this insures the owner against the actions of dishonest employees
- personal accident and sickness; to recover income lost through inability to work
- hospital expenses
- motor insurance (private and commercial)
- burglary; this only includes *breaking* and entering
- *all-risks*; a wide cover which incorporates many of the above, i.e. it is insurance to refund *any* loss or damage
- money loss
- goods in transit; goods being moved
- employer's liability; against being sued by an employee who is injured at work

- public liability; as employer's, but for members of the public (e.g. the postman)
- products liability; in case your product harms or causes loss to anyone
- boilers; in case of boiler explosion
- professional indemnities; in case you are sued for professional incompetence
- glass; for example, shop-windows
- libel; in case you accidently write something damaging about someone, for example, in advertisements
- licence; if your business depends on you having some licence
- credit; in case your debtors don't pay
- contract; if you are dependent on some contract being fulfilled
- contingency; to insure against some event happening, like not inheriting some money.

When taking out insurance, remember that any information withheld or wrongly stated to the insurance company (the *insurer*) will stop you (the *insured*) from receiving your money. You will usually be given a suggestion or sample form (a *proposal*) first, and then when you reach agreement you will be given the proper thing (the *policy*) in writing. Store it at your bank.

You are only allowed to insure something you have an economic advantage in preserving.

Some insurances are intended to reimburse you only with amounts lost (an indemnity), whilst others are merely to provide you with a lump sum (like a gamble).

If the insurance company pays up, it can sue on your behalf to reclaim its 'loss', with or without your consent.

Action Guidelines

1 Small firms should be able to enjoy the advantage of lower, well-controlled costs. Is yours such a firm?

2 When did you last check on your insurance cover? Have there been any changes in your firm to warrant extra, or less, insurance?

3 Find the time to compare this year's bills for electricity, gas, telephones and water rates against those for the corresponding periods last year. Satisfy yourself that there are good reasons for any dramatic changes.

13

Buying Fixed Assets

- **Asset purchases determine the long-term structure and objectives of a firm.**
- **Purchase decisions can be helped by knowing the payback period and the annual rate of return.**
- **Microcomputers can help.**
- **The purchase of assets must allow for tax, depreciation, running costs and interest charges.**

Types of fixed assets

From time to time you will have to buy large items like machines, furniture, cars and lorries, and you will have to decide whether these items are worth buying or leasing. These large assets fall into one of four types.

Type A: assets like tables, buildings and signs, of which you cannot easily measure the benefit.

Type B: assets like cars, lorries and some machines. The more you are willing to pay initially, the less should be the machine's running costs. So, for a car, are you better off (1) buying one that has a low purchase price, but *higher* running costs, or (2) one that costs more at first, but has *lower* running costs?

Type C: assets that clearly and measurably *save* you costs. For example, a photocopier, typewriter or microcomputer might save you staff costs. You can therefore compare the purchase prices of these with the savings they bring.

Type D: assets that will bring you sales income. For example, a welding machine may enable you to offer customers a new service. Thus you can compare the initial purchase price with the sales income expected.

Assets type A

Accounting methods cannot help much with these assets. You must use your judgement in coming to a decision, compromising quality with cost considerations. The quality required will partly depend on the impression the asset will leave with your customer.

Assets type B

Accounting methods can help you with these assets. You have to be very careful when buying cars and lorries, because the suppliers spend millions of pounds trying to make you forget the costs and think only of your image.

- *Rule* 1 *must be* not to buy your cars in the UK. Belgium seems to be the best place. You can get details of how to import a private car from the Consumers' Association, publishers of *Which? Car* magazine.

  The rules are easier for importing one car privately, than to import for resale. If you can't get a right-hand drive, the cost of converting a car from left-hand drive to right-hand drive is of the order of £40 or less.
- *Rule* 2 *might be* to buy one-year-old cars, because the cost of virginity in cars is high! Naturally you will have to give special attention to the sort of usage the car has had. Cars used for demonstration *can* be good value.
- *Rule* 3 *might be* to keep the car to the end of its reasonable life. This will be elaborated on when we talk about rates of depreciation. The idea of changing cars every two years came from the manufacturers.
- *Rule* 4 *must be* to give primary consideration to the rate of depreciation of the car. How many years will it last? What will it be worth in five years' time?

$$\% \text{ depreciation} = \frac{\text{purchase price} - \text{sale price in 5 years}}{\text{purchase price}} \times 100$$

You should be able to discover the five-year-old sale value from newspaper advertisements or one of the published guides.

Purchase price versus running costs How can you compare purchase prices with running costs?

We shall assume that a car costs £5000, does 40 miles per gallon, and has an average annual service cost of £200. The estimated useful life of the car (a company car) is five years. The average price of a gallon of fuel will be £2.50 over the next five years. The estimated annual mileage is 25,000 miles. The car is purchased with a two-year bank loan at 15 per cent per year interest:

	£
Annual portion of price (£5000 ÷ 5)	1000
Annual petrol cost (25,000 miles × (£2.50 ÷ 40))	1563
Annual service cost	200
Annual interest charge (£5000 × 15% × 2 yr ÷ 5 yr)	300
Total annual cost =	£3063

Compare the above car with another costing £6000 but giving 50 miles per gallon. The tax and insurance costs are the same as for the £5000 car:

	£
Annual purchase price charge (£6000 ÷ 5)	1200
Annual petrol cost (25,000 × (£2.50 ÷ 50))	1250
Annual service cost	200
Annual interest charge (£6000 × 15% × 2 ÷ 5)	360
Total annual costs =	£3010

There is not a lot in it, but the £6000 car is cheaper in this case, largely because of the better petrol consumption figure.

The most uncertain figure in the above is the price of petrol. We might, therefore, turn the calculations around by asking the question, '*at what price of petrol does the 50 m.p.g. car become cheaper*?' From Table M we can see that it would not be worth buying the higher priced car unless the price of petrol reached about £2.10.

Table M

Petrol price:	**£1.80**		**£2.20**		**£2.50**	
Car:	**40 m.p.g.**	**50 m.p.g.**	**40 m.p.g.**	**50 m.p.g.**	**40 m.p.g.**	**50 m.p.g.**
Price	1000	1200	1000	1200	1000	1200
Petrol	1125	900	1375	1100	1563	1250
Service	200	200	200	200	200	200
Interest	300	360	300	360	300	360
	2625	2660	2875	2860	3063	3010

Machines We could use the same approach to find the costs necessary to equate two production machines. Here petrol would be replaced by oil or electricity and the choice is between buying an expensive, fast machine or a cheaper, slower one – see Table N.

Table N

	Machine Ordinary	*Machine Superfast*
Purchase price	£11,000	£14,000
Maintenance	£300/year	£700/year
Electricity	£2000/year	£2500/year
Life span	5 years	5 years
Scrap value	nil	nil
Interest	15% for 5 years	15% for 5 years
Profit/unit made	£0.70	£0.70

We can ask the question 'how many *more* per year will the super machine have to make in order to make its extra costs worth while?':

	Machine Ordinary	*Machine Superfast*
	£	£
Annual price charge	2200	2800
Annual maintenance	300	700
Annual electricity	2000	2500
Annual interest	1650	2100
Totals	6150	8100

The difference is £1950, so that with an extra profit per unit of £0.70, the extra number required to equate the costs of the machines is 2785 units.

Assets type C

These are the assets you buy to save costs. This should cause you few problems – it is just a matter of comparing costs with savings. Do not forget to include (*a*) interest, (*b*) running and maintenance costs, (*c*) employers' NI contributions, and (*d*) staff facilities costs.

You will have to include an interest charge even if you do not actually pay any. This is because when you buy something, you forgo the chance to put the purchase price in a deposit account and earn the interest on it. Always assume you are *borrowing* the purchase price of a new asset.

Payback period It may also be worth your while working out how *long* it will be before your savings exceed your costs. For example, if you buy a welder to replace some part-time staff:

	£	
Automatic welder	8000	(including interest)
Maintenance	400	
	£8400	

If the part-time wages saved are £2500, the welder will have paid for itself (*payback*) in 3.36 years.

For small firms, with potential cash problems, payback periods of two years may be the maximum allowed. While you are waiting two years for the cost savings to start showing, the project is a drain on your cash.

Assets type D

These assets will bring a measurable income to the firm.

Assume you are deciding between buying a milling machine and a lathe. With either you could offer a service to your customers, thus making a separate identifiable profit with each. Clearly all you have to do is (1) work out the total profit each will earn you over the life of the asset, and (2) subtract the costs.

Do not forget the interest charges, and it may be useful, from your cash point of view, again to consider the payback period. If, say, the lathe's payback period is much shorter than the milling machine's, this may be more important than the small net profit advantage that the milling machine earns.

Annual rate of return Another figure that may be useful is one called the *annual rate of return.* This can be worked out as follows:

	£	
Purchase price of machine	20,000	
Sales income from machine per year	60,000	
Machine costs per year	54,000	(including interest)
Profit per year	6,000	

$$\text{Annual rate of return} = \frac{£6,000}{£20,000} \times 100 = 30\%$$

This is like saying that the machine earns a 30% profit each year.

Financing assets

Leasing If you *lease* an asset you *never* own it. So you can lease a machine for many years, then the leasor will come along and take it back. If you decide to *buy* its replacement, you may even end up buying the one you'd been leasing for years! Leasors do not (usually) allow you to buy out the lease for anything less than the total rentals you would eventually have to pay them anyway. A lease is a legal contract to pay the rentals agreed. Failure to pay could lead to court action against you to pay the balance (see later).

You can *buy* (own) an asset using your firm's money, by a bank loan, or by hire purchase.

Hire purchase With hire purchase you become the owner only after you have made the final payment. If you default, the HP company will take the asset away and leave you nothing to show for your previous payments.

With HP, usually, the firm supplying the goods sells the goods to a finance company, which hires it to you. When you have paid the last instalment, the finance company has sold the goods to you.

Hire purchase is expensive – that is, the interest rates charged are high. Also, you cannot get cash discounts from the supplier, because these are offered because a cash sale saves the supplier a lot of the paperwork connected with HP.

Bank loan With a bank loan you own the asset immediately. On default of payment to the bank, the bank will collect on whatever you have pledged as security. A problem you *will* come up against is how to compare bank and finance house interest rates.

If you buy using HP you will be charged a rate of interest based on the initial price. For example:

Equipment cost	£1000
HP interest rate	12% over three years
Total charge	£1000 + (£1000 × 12% × 3) = £1360

The monthly repayments would therefore be £37.77.

If you had bought the equipment using a bank *overdraft*, you would only pay interest on the amount of the loan outstanding. Thus (approximately):

Initial balance outstanding	£1000
Final balance outstanding	£0
Average balance outstanding	£500
Interest charged on balance	12% × £500 = £60 per year
Total debt	£1000 + (3 × 60) = £1180
Monthly repayments (approx.)	$\frac{1180}{36}$ = £32.77

So, **check if your interest rates are charged against the initial amount *or* the outstanding balance due.**

Which loan type? Long-term assets (e.g. building and machinery) must be paid for with long-term cash (e.g. HP). Short-term assets (e.g. stock and debtors) are best paid for with short-term cash (e.g. creditors and overdrafts).

In other words, do not buy your fixed assets (such as machines) using money that may be recalled by the lender at very short notice. If you do buy machines with an overdraft, and the bank calls back this loan, you will have to sell the machine in a hurry to find the cash.

Tax The taxman *will* let you charge *lease rentals* to your profit and loss account (like electricity). But he *won't* let you charge *HP payments*, because he treats these like the *purchase* of an asset. He thus only allows the depreciation of it into the profit and loss account. He has his own depreciation rates, described in the next section.

Depreciation rates

In Unit 6 we explained that the difference between the intitial (higher) price and the present (lower) price was the *accumulated* depreciation.

Some people do not use the 'estimate the resale price' method. Rather, they use more 'mechanical' methods. These include the following.

The Straight-Line Method

Storage container costs	£2000
Scrap value	£200 after 5 years
Monthly depreciation	$\frac{£2000 - £200}{5 \times 12}$ = £30 each and every month

This method should only be used on assets whose depreciation is primarily dependent on the passage of time. That is, the resale value of the storage container was mainly dependent on how old it was, not on how much use it had seen.

Production-hour method

Machine costs	£2000	
Scrap value after it has run for 10,400 hours	£200	
Hourly depreciation	$\frac{£1800}{10,400}$	=£0.173
This month's run	130 hours	
This month's depreciation	£22.49	

This method is used on assets whose resale values are mainly dependent upon how many hours (or miles, etc.) they have been worked.

Reducing-balance method

Car costs	£5000
Estimated life of the car	5 years

Here we apply a percentage figure to the *written-down value* (cost – accumulated depreciation). For an asset with about a five-year life, the percentage will be about 40 per cent per year. (This percentage was found by saying: It would take 20 per cent a year for five years to reduce £5000 to NIL. The written-down value will average half the cost, i.e. £2500. It will take twice 20 per cent of depreciation on £2500 to get £5000 to nil in five years.) This is very approximate, and is explained in more detail in Table O.

Table O

Year	Cost	Accumulated depreciation	Written-down value
0	5000	nil	5000
1		40% × £5000 = 2000	3000
2		40% × £3000 = 1200	1800
3		40% × £1800 = 720	1080 etc.

The idea behind this rather messy method is that the asset gets heavily depreciated in its first few years, less so in later years. This seems reasonable for a car.

You must remember that these calculations were invented by accountants working in large firms who could not value the assets by just estimating their market values. These mechanical methods are often sadly astray.

The taxman's method The taxman ignores your depreciation methods. He has his own complicated methods. He is not concerned with a nice even annual profit figure. He has, though, been told to encourage your capital expenditure, i.e. expenditure on assets whose lives run into years.

Before he applies his tax percentage, he will redraft your profit and loss account. This redraft includes changing your depreciation method to his. For example, he writes all machines off in the first year! Thus, in the year you buy an asset, your company's tax bill on profits drops significantly. *You* would be unwise to use the taxman's depreciation methods - they distort your profit figure badly.

Computers

One large purchase decision you may be concerned with is whether to buy a small computer to do your accounts for you. We will now turn our attention to this problem.

Small (usually called *micro*) computers are used by some small companies in the production of their goods. Examples include weighing machines, cash registers, stock records, and even to assist in motor car servicing.

QUESTION: Should I buy a computer to help me do my accounts?

ANSWER: No, not unless you have some previous experience to call on.

All right, you insist on going further. I warn you, computers can take up more of your time than the rest of your business put together.

QUESTION: What sort of computers are there?

ANSWER: (1) The big ones called mainframes, (2) the *micro* home computers (mainly for games), and (3) the *micro* business systems. Purchase prices (and that's the half of it) for each type respectively go, £½ million, £500, £6000. The one that interests you is number (3), and only number (3)!

QUESTION: What does *micro* business system mean?

ANSWER: *Micro* means built using very small circuit boards, called *micro* processors, which were a massive cost breakthrough some years ago. *Business system* means that the equipment has been especially designed with a medium to small sized business in mind. They are capable of doing invoicing, wages, double-entry book-keeping, etc.

QUESTION: What does *equipment* include?

ANSWER: Computer equipment is broadly divided into (1) *hardware*, and (2) *software*. The former includes the electronic circuits, the video screen and the keyboard. The software is the instructions to the computer on what to do. These include such things as whether the computer should add, print, multiply, or await the operator's next command. Software comes on cassette tapes or discs (like gramophone records) and is played into the hardware before the system can be used.

QUESTION: Which is more important, hardware or software?

ANSWER: Despite the fact you usually get approached initially by the hardware manufacturers, *what you must consider first is the software.* You should thus first find the set of programmed instructions (software) that suits *you.* This done, buy the hardware that the software was designed for. Do not listen to advice to buy the software from one supplier and the equipment (hardware) from another supplier. It can be a case of 'penny-wise, pound-foolish'.

QUESTION: What's this hardware again?

ANSWER: It's the equipment you see when you are looking at a microcomputer. The software is the invisible bit that controls the machine. Look at Figure 11. This is how

Figure 11 A typical microcomputer office set-up. The hardware includes (1) the circuit board known as the *processor*, (2) a keyboard, (3) a machine to drive the software discs, known as a disc-drive, (4) a visual display unit (VDU) which looks like a television screen, and (5) a paper printer.

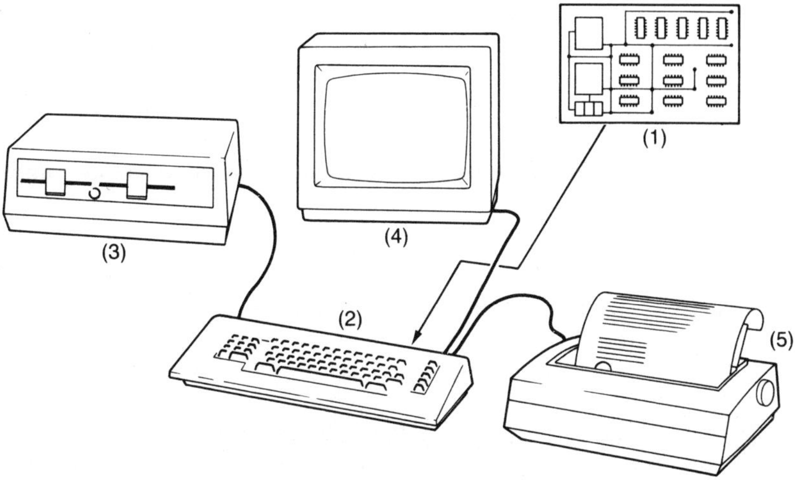

it works. (*a*) The instruction set (software) on the discs go into the *disc drive.* When run, this tells the *circuit board* what to do. (*b*) When it is necessary for you to provide the machine with a number or command, you do so using the *keyboard.* (*c*) When the circuit board has some calculation to show you it can either show it on the screen or, if you want a copy to take away, (*d*) it will print the results via the *printer.*

QUESTION: You say all this will do my general ledger, cash book, sales ledger, wages, etc, and it costs £6000?

ANSWER: No, the hardware costs about £6000 initially, the software will cost you about another £2000. You have also to pay for (1) maintenance, say £500 per year, (2) paper, (3) discs, (4) electricity, and (5) typewriter ribbons. But most of all, someone will have sit in front of it for long periods telling it what to do. For example, telling it the invoice amounts and names, the hours Mr Smith worked this week, and who has paid you what.

QUESTION: How would I go about looking at one; that is, looking for the software that would suit me?

ANSWER: Firstly, don't bother with the computer companies' displays for now. Find a friend or associate in a similar sized firm and in a similar industry, and look at his software. Learn from *his* mistakes! If you don't know anyone with a micro, go to your local computer shop. State your interest in business systems, and ask for the name of sorneone you can visit *alone*; that is, a reference from them.

QUESTION: I've seen microcomputers advertised for £60; what about those?

ANSWER: Consider them as toys. Computers are measured in k's. It's a bit like cc's in a car engine. A business system needs at least 48k, which the smaller micros cannot provide.

It also needs to be a machine that can use discs and can print 80 letters across one line (on screen or printer). The £60–£1000 machines can't do this. They were designed for games, students and teachers. You might buy one as an elaborate calculator, but not as a keeper of your accounts.

QUESTION: What about deals, discounts, obsolescence, second-hand, etc?

ANSWER: Don't bother with deals that mean you get no after-sales service. Buy the lot *straight* from a local supplier, if necessary paying a bit over the odds for local service and advice. Once you've decided to buy a system, put yourself into the hands of your local agent. The advantage here is that you can always ring him up after the purchase, for help. **After sales service is of paramount importance.**

QUESTION: Is there any way I can use a computer to do my accounts, but subcontract the workings to someone else?

ANSWER: Yes, this might be a good idea. The thing you're looking for is a *computer bureau.* They can be a good introduction to computing. Look in your 'yellow pages' for your local one.

A word of warning. These bureaux are run by the real experts. The systems they run could get you to the moon! Don't let them give you more record keeping than you really need. If you are choosing between bureaux, decide on the one that does what *you* want, not the one that tells you what you must do to use *its* systems. A good bureau will be able to offer you a system which, when running, appears to you tailor-made. START SIMPLE - ADD EXTRA FACILITIES LATER.

A perfectly working, computerized accounting system would be a dream. Unfortunately, like most things in life, perfection rarely exists!

Action Guidelines

1 The purchase of a fixed asset is a major decision which will affect the image, development and flexibility of your firm. You cannot always make such a decision using only financial criteria - a great deal of managerial judgement is necessary. Having decided that a machine or whatever is really necessary, you must then decide which is the most appropriate way of paying for it.

2 When using financial data to help you make a decision about a new item, include only relevant costs, think hard about hidden costs, clearly identify the important running costs, and know *why* you are buying.

3 Microcomputers are now available at prices which should make every manager consider their relevance. You should discover what is available even if you are convinced that your present systems are efficient. Do not dismiss them out of hand, and do not install one for the sake of being *modern.*

14

Budgeting

- **Budgeting is essential even to small firms.**
- **Operations are not under control unless there is first a plan.**
- **Plans should only be as detailed as they need to be.**
- **A budget is a financial plan.**

Why plan?

The word 'manager' suggests the arranging of people and machines to take best advantage of the future. 'Why plan?' is like saying 'why manage?'

When we looked at how to calculate your profit and loss account, we were talking about *things in the past.* What about the future? Surely the *future* profit and loss account is more important than the historical one.

- Is it worth my continuing in business?
- What problems am I about to face?

These are questions a good *manager* should ask himself.

Forecasting

Forecasting *is* possible. It becomes less certain the more precise you try to make it, and with the distance into the future you are forecasting. But it is better to have forecasted and failed by 10 per cent, than never to have forecasted at all!

You *can* have a good guess at the prices you will pay and have to charge over the next year. You know what sort of profit you want, so you can set yourself a target sales income figure. All this done, you can produce a *planned* profit and loss account.

'Planned' means more than 'forecasted'. A plan you *make* happen; a forecast is what will happen without any effort from you. Once a financial plan has been settled for your firm, it is the *budget.*

Starting point

How do you go about planning a profit and loss account?

First you need to figure out how much profit you are willing to accept for next year. This budgeted profit will include some for you, some for reinvestment.

Next figure out what could stop you getting that profit. Is it the hours you are willing to work, is it the amount you can sell, or is it the number of jobs you will get? The 'thing' that might stop you getting your budgeted profit is called your *limiting factor.*

Limiting factor

This is what limits your profit. It is often the number of orders received, but not always. You might not want to grow, so your limiting factor will be the number of hours you are *willing* to make available.

If there is you, and two helpers each working 40-hour weeks, then output will be limited to 120 hours per week.

Some firms are limited by the availability of materials, by a machine's speed, or by the size of a factory. These too can be limiting factors.

Steps to budget profit and loss account

For the *production-line* company the budget profit and loss account will be compiled as in Figure 12. Let us go through it. (Box names will be emphasized.)

Figure 12 Steps in fixing a budget profit and loss account.

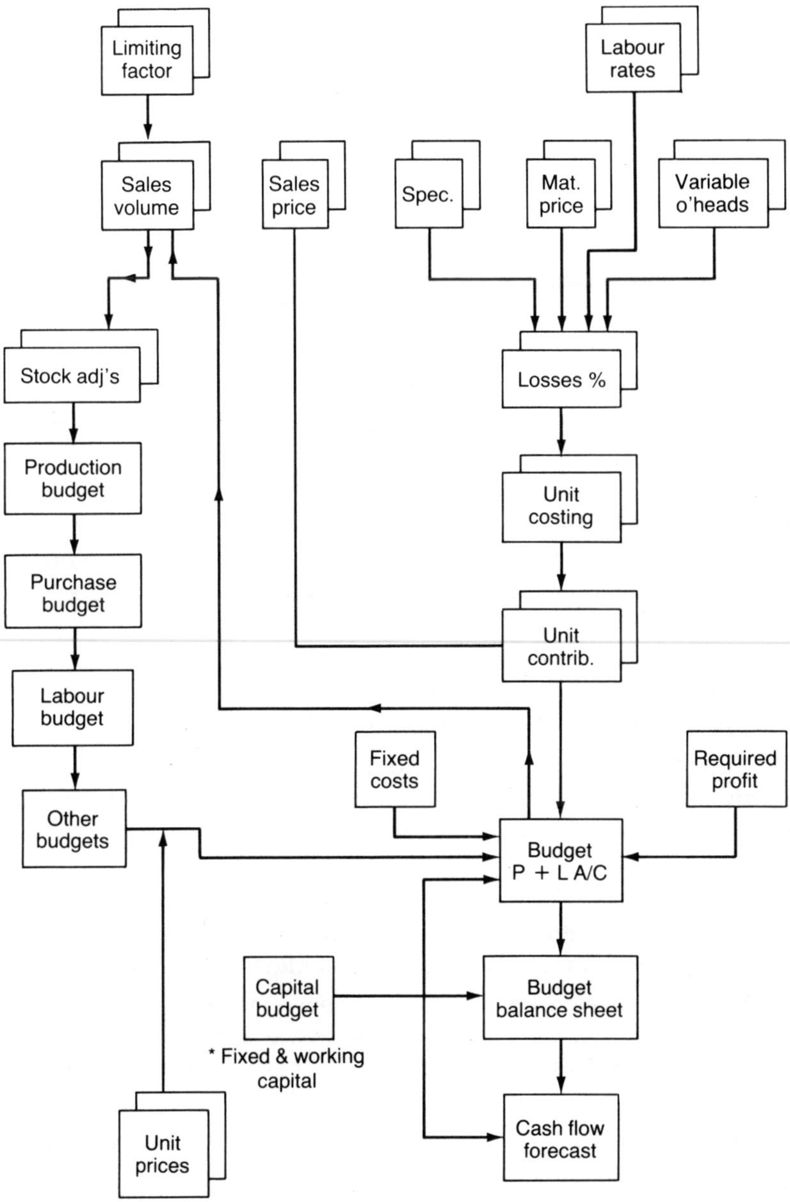

1. Find the box with *limiting factor* in it. Here we shall assume *sales volume* is the limiting factor. On the right you will see *sales price.* You will need to forecast your average sales prices for the next year.
2. Compile a product *specification* or recipe. If the specification can vary use a most likely specification; failing that, use a 'most expensive' specification.
3. Forecast the average *material price* per unit.
4. Forecast the *variable overheads,* such as packaging.
5. Cost your specification per unit allowing for *losses.* Such losses include those in storage, those in production, and those for samples.
6. Take the difference between your *unit costing* and the forecasted *sales price*, and thus know your *contribution* towards fixed costs per unit.
7. Forecast your expenditure on each of your *fixed costs* (e.g. interest, advertising, salaries).
8. Calculate your depreciation charges from your *capital budget.* This is a plan of the machines, lorries, etc. (fixed assets) you intend to buy in the near future.
9. Using the unit contribution, fixed costs including depreciation, and the required profit, calculate how many units you must sell to reach your *sales volume* target.
10. You should now be able to prepare a statement of what quantity needs to be produced (a *production budget*); of what quantity needs to be purchased (*purchase budget*); and how many hours will have to be worked (*labour budget*). *Other budgets* may also be calculated as you see fit.
11. As a check, put costs to your budgets, and subtract the sales income. You should be able to recalculate your required profit.
12. You should also be able to forecast your year-end *balance sheet*, and in a later unit we shall do the forecasted *cash flow* statement. (This shows how much cash you will need and when.)
13. Having done all this for the year ahead, subdivide this total budget into twelve monthly budgets.

A specimen budget

Let us assume that Cooking Items Company makes two pan types: frying pans and milk pans. The required annual profit is £6000. Experience shows that their sales are divided into 60 per cent milk pans and 40 per cent frying pans. A one per cent settlement discount is given. The company also estimates:

	Frying pans	*Milk pans*
Sales price	£2 each	£3 each
Finished goods stock		
Starting stock	1000	1100
Year-end stock	1200	900
Raw materials used		
Plastic	1lb	0 at £0.30/lb
Aluminium	2lb	2lb at £0.20/lb
Fittings (each)	0	3 at £0.15
Labour		
Junior	2 hours	0
Foreman	1 hour	1 hour
Other	0	3 hours
Packaging	£0.10	£0.10

Other estimates are:

(*a*) estimated finished goods losses are two per cent of sales volume
(*b*) estimated materials losses are five per cent of production quantity
(*c*) closing material stocks are required to be equal to 10 per cent of the production quantity
(*d*) opening material stocks are estimated to be: plastic 936lb, aluminium 4590lb, fittings 4077
(*e*) the total of the fixed cost is estimated to be £7000
(*f*) the wage bill will total £27,647.

So we can first work out the *unit costings*, as shown in Table P.

At this point we can calculate the total number of pans to be sold (N):

Fixed cost + Labour + Profit = (Frying pan contribution × N × 40%) + (Milk pan contribution × N × 60%)

Table P		Frying pans		Milk pans
		£		£
Plastic	1.05 × 1lb × £0.30 =	0.3150		
Aluminium	1.05 × 2lb × £0.20 =	0.4200	1.05 × 2 × £0.20 =	0.4200
Fittings		0	1.05 × 3 × £0.15 =	0.4725
		0.7350		0.8925
Packaging		0.1000		0.1000
Total variable costs before losses		0.8350		0.9925
Finished goods losses (2%)		0.0167		0.0199
Total variable costs		0.8517		1.0124
Sales price		2.0000		3.0000
		1.1483		1.9876
Less settlement discount		0.0200		0.0300
Contribution per unit		1.1283		1.9576

That is

$$7000 + 27647 + 6000 = (1.1283 \times N \times 0.4) + (1.9576 \times N \times 0.6)$$
$$40647 = (0.45132 + 1.17456)N$$
$$N = 25{,}000 \text{ pans}$$

Out of the 25,000 total, 40 per cent (10,000) are frying pans and 60 per cent (15,000) are milk pans. *These are therefore the target sales of each.*

The next questions are:

(*a*) what quantities of materials will the firm need to buy?
(*b*) how many labour hours will be required?
(*c*) how many pans will it need to *make* (allowing for the change in stock levels)?

Obviously we now need production, materials and labour budgets.

Production budget

	Frying pans	*Milk pans*
Opening stock	1,000	1,100
Production (balance)	?	?
Less closing stock	(1,200)	(900)
Less losses (2%)	(200)	(300)
To sales	10,000	15,000

To make the columns balance, the missing figures must be 10,400 and 15,100.

Materials budget

	Plastic (lb)	*Aluminium (lb)*	*Fittings (each)*
Opening stock	936	4,590	4,077
Purchases required	?	?	?
Less closing stock	(1,040)	(5,100)	(4,530)
Less losses	(520)	(2,550)	(2,265)
For frying pans	10,400	20,800	0
Milk pans	0	30,200	45,300
To production	10,400	51,000	45,300

Again, to make the columns balance the missing figures must be 11,024lb plastic, 54,060lb aluminium, and 48,018 fittings.

Labour budget

	Junior	*Foreman*	*Other*
For frying pans	20,800 hours	10,400 hours	0 hours
For milk pans	0 hours	15,100 hours	45,300 hours
	20,800 hours	25,500 hours	45,300 hours

This now means we have determined the materials to be bought, the hours of labour needed, and the numbers of pans to *make*!

Jobbing and services companies

For jobbing and services companies the task of budgeting is very easy. All you have to do is:

1. total the estimated annual fixed overheads and wages (say £60,000)
2. add on the required profit (say £15,000)
3. decide on a rate per hour to charge customers (say £9.00 per hour)
4. work out how many hours of jobs you and the staff *must do*:
   $\frac{£75{,}000}{£9}$ = 8333 hours = 160 hours per week.

Action Guidelines

1 Always start a plan by clearly identifying your limiting factors.

2 Do not be satisfied with the first plan you work out. Try adjusting your estimates to see how the profit is affected, always remembering your limiting factors. Remember also that your budget for the year, once decided, *should not be changed during the year.* It is a *target.* (If an archer consistently fires to the left of his target it would serve no useful purpose to move the target to the left - he must readjust his aim!)

3 Be realistic in setting the limiting factors. (If the same archer consistently fires short of the target, it *could* serve a useful purpose to move the target closer to start with!)

15

Controlling Your Working Capital

- **You need to invest in stocks and labour before you trade. These costs must be kept to a minimum.**
- **How long is your operating cycle?**
- **Cheques are not identical to cash – the difference is three or four days. Time is money.**
- **With inflation, forecasting your cash needs is crucial.**

The ideal would be to have no money invested in a company and still be earning a profit!

Unfortunately, only some service industries (e.g. agencies) can get anywhere near this perfect state. Retailers, wholesalers and many service industries do not invest in any expensive machinery but still earn a good living for the owners.

If you are deciding which type of company to invest in you might consider this. If you are decided on your type of industry, then you should try to run the business with as little capital invested as possible. You should not under-invest, but nor should you over-invest. This is not just a question of whether to buy or lease, but rather of whether a good profit can be made without a particular asset.

Retailers and service industries do often require higher quality non-machinery assets such as premises. Retailers need to finance a large range of stock. Manufacturers, on the other hand, have that heavy commitment to machinery and product developments, an unenviable position.

If you are a manufacturer it is better to have

- your money invested in machinery (earning profits) than in stocks - provided your machines are being fully used
- your money invested in debtors (at least you have sold the goods) than as stocks - assuming your debtors will pay on time

It is a waste of money having cash balances, unless it is earning interest as an investment.

Working capital

The money you have invested in *stock, debtors* and *cash,* less any money you owe for *current liabilities* (e.g. creditors), is called your WORKING CAPITAL.

It is called 'working' because it is constantly changing from cash to goods, to cash again. Some people call it NET NEAR-CASH - 'net' because you subtract the liabilities, 'near-cash' because that is just what (you hope) it is, cash you can use to pay creditors. If there is any left over, you get it!

People looking at your profit and loss account to see how you are doing (such as bank managers) will take special interest in your working capital. This is because, in the absence of a cash forecast, it's the next best thing.

Generally, it is considered right to have *twice as much in current assets (stock, debtors, cash) as you have in current liabilities (creditors).*

If you have *less than twice*, this means you may be pushed to pay creditors! If you have *more than twice*, this means you may be over-investing in stocks and debtors!

Let us look at a sample balance sheet:

Part balance sheet

	£	£
Current assets		
Raw material stock	8,000	
WIP stock	2,000	
Finished goods stock	14,000	
Debtors	25,500	
Cash	500	
		50,000
Less *current liabilities*		
Creditors	(13,000)	
Tax	(9,000)	
		(22,000)
Working capital		28,000

We know also that the annual sales were £300,000, the annual purchases were £210,000, and the cost of goods sold was £250,000. We can therefore work out how many weeks of stocks, debtors and creditors the firm holds.

Operating cycle

Let us consider the *timing* of a manufacturing business, that is its *operating cycle.*

- we borrow money from a bank charging interest daily
- we put money into raw material stock, probably getting a month's credit
- we need more *time* actually to make the goods
- we have to waste *time* holding finished goods
- we have to allow more *time* for the customer to pay
- we get our cash back

The longer it takes to complete the cycle, the more interest you have to pay, and the more capital you need to run the business. The firm in the balance sheet above had £28,000 invested in this operating cycle.

The size of your operating cycle investment will be the result of your efficiency, and your type of business. A wine manufacturer can have a cycle that is *years* long. Thus, wine making is left to Barons! A cash chemist only has raw material stock, has no machinery, has no debtors, and will have a lot of creditors (credit purchases). Its operating cycle will be measured in days.

So let us now use the figures to calculate the operating cycle of our example firm:

			Weeks
1 *Time* spent as raw materials	$= \dfrac{\text{stock level}}{\text{purchases per week}}$	$= \dfrac{8000}{4038}$	= 1.98
2 *Time* saved by having credit purchases	$= \dfrac{\text{creditors}}{\text{purchases per week}}$	$= \dfrac{13{,}000}{4038}$	= (3.22)
3 *Time* spent in production (WIP)	$= \dfrac{\text{WIP}}{\text{COGS per week}}$	$= \dfrac{2000}{4807}$	= 0.41
4 *Time* spent in finished goods	$= \dfrac{\text{stock}}{\text{sales per week}}$	$= \dfrac{14{,}000}{5769}$	= 2.42
5 *Time* spent in debtors	$= \dfrac{\text{debtors}}{\text{sales per week}}$	$= \dfrac{25{,}500}{5769}$	= 4.42
Total operating cycle			6.01

It takes this firm a little over six weeks to extract the profit it makes on its investment in men and materials. In a year it thus gets

$\dfrac{52}{6}$ = 8.66 'attempts' to make a profit.

Suppose that an enlightened manager of this firm decides to stop being so fast paying his creditors. He decides not to pay any of them until the end of the month following the delivery. On average that is six weeks:

$$6 \text{ weeks} = \frac{\text{creditors (?)}}{\text{purchases per week}}$$

$\therefore$ creditors = 6 × 4038 = £24,228

The balance sheet now looks like this:

	£	£
Current assets		50,000
Less *current liabilities*		
Creditors	(24,228)	
Tax	(9,000)	
		(33,228)
WORKING CAPITAL		16,772

The working capital has been reduced, which is good, but there is now a ratio of current assets to current liabilities of

$$\frac{50,000}{33,228} = 1.5$$

That's not the *twice* suggested as ideal! The firm may be accused of being in a postion of not being able to pay its liabilities. It's a hard life!

If you want to reduce your working capital (i.e. your operating cycle):

- concentrate on your stocks and debtors first
- only increase your creditors after you have improved your stocks and debtors.

Controlling stock, debtors and creditors

Stock

- Have regular stock-takes.
- Ensure good co-ordination between tasks, such as between buying and production.
- Get rid of obsolete stock quickly.
- Have good stock records.
- Give nearly as much thought to delivery times as to price when ordering.

Debtors

- Invoice customers quickly.

- Get as many customers to pay cash as possible.
- Have a rigorous, direct, debt-collection routine.
- Have good, neat sales ledger records, probably analysed into 'months overdue'.
- Avoid bad payers by checking up on them first (see later).

Creditors
- Delay paying as long as you dare.
- Always buy on the longest credit terms available.
- Ignore settlement discount offers of *less than* 2½ per cent.
- If you don't take the discount don't pay for another month.

You will notice that good working capital management suggests a reversal of normal morals. Borrow as much as you can and delay paying it back. Do not lend money to debtors, but if you do, continually harass them for its return.

More about debtors

Do not give credit unless you have to, or if you feel it will increase your sales.

There are several things you need to know about your credit customers. These details can be kept on their sales ledger cards. You must have:

(a) their business *name* in full
(b) the address of their *registered* office
(c) the address and phone number of the place that keeps their purchase ledger
(d) their bank and branch
(e) their VAT and company number
(f) the names of the directors or proprietors
(g) when they started trading, and in what
(h) copies of their past profit and loss account and balance sheet
(i) the name of their auditors
(j) the names of some other firms giving them credit (ring these up for a reference)
(k) the registration numbers of their vehicles visiting you.

You may not be able to get all this, but do get as much as you can.

When you have a bad debt you'll wish you'd tried harder!

With new accounts, set a limit on how much you expect them to owe you at any one time.

Do not send them statements (photocopies of your sales ledger record), unless there is some problem. Write 'no statement supplied' on your invoice. You may even write 'Please note, interest on overdue accounts is 5% monthly' on your invoices. Whether you enforce this or not is up to you.

Avoid getting unreconciled sums of money. For example, if your ledger shows £212 owing for August and £130 owing for September, and you receive a cheque for £150, 'phone immediately for an explanation. Discourage the practice – it is the first step to a bad debt.

Make good use of the telephone once you have sent an overdue notice. This is more direct, more personal. Threaten, politely, to phone every day! *Don't get a reputation for sending five overdue notices!* Keep smiling even when you take them to court. Remember they may make a comeback!

Use the County Court procedure for 'bad debts' under £2000. You will need a good file on all the details of a bad debtor. However, admit to yourself when you have been robbed, and do not waste money chasing a debtor who has no money.

You may FACTOR your sales ledger to someone else (see Unit 17).

Forecasting for cash

Many well-known firms (for example, Laker Airways, Rolls-Royce) have had good products, but have been stopped from trading because they ran out of ready cash.

It is important to know how much cash you *will* have in the future. Look at your bank statements over the last few months to see the fluctuations which can occur.

You can control your cash balance (to some extent) by forecasting what your future expenditures and incomes are likely to be. Do a *cash flow forecast.* It will help you and impress those who lend you money!

How do you do it?
First, take up your forecasted *monthly* profit and loss account.

Secondly, make a list down the left side of a sheet of paper of
all your sources of income
all your expenditures (as below)

Thirdly, across the top of the page write the names of the months (we are doing a *monthly* cash forecast).

Fourthly, fill in the amounts you expect to pay or receive, *when it actually hits your bank account*, under the appropriate months.

If you are *giving* one month's credit on your sales, then allow one month's delay between the time of the sale (shown on the profit and loss account) and the cash received (shown on the cash forecast).

As for sales, if you are *taking* one month's credit on purchases allow a month's delay between the purchase shown on the profit and loss account, and on the cash flow forecast.

Remember that the ratios

$$\frac{\text{debtors}}{\text{sales per month}} \times 12 \quad \text{and} \quad \frac{\text{creditors}}{\text{purchase per month}} \times 12$$

will tell you how many months' credit you are *actually* giving and taking, respectively.

Put in the purchases of large assets (capital expenditure) under the months when you will actually pay for them.

Include VAT, PAYE, drawings - everything.

The result Table Q shows a possible cash flow summary. For this company its overall cash balance is expected to change from a £40,000 overdraft to a £12,000 credit balance.

If its overdraft limit was set as £60,000, it would have problems in April and May. These problems could easily be overcome by moving the £63,000 capital expenditure to after the summer season.

The adjustment was easy when we had the information!

Bank managers like to know you do cash flow forecasts. When making loans they may insist on one.

Table Q An example (brackets mean outflows or overdraft)

1983 (£000s)	Dec '82	Jan '83	Feb	Mar	Apr	May	Jun	July	Aug	Sept	Oct	Nov	Dec	Jan '84
INFLOWS														
Sales cash received		30	32	34	33	47	62	74	81	30	30	30	30	
Sales of assets						14					6			
Loans received					53					53				
Sub-total		30	32	34	86	61	62	74	81	83	36	30	30	
OUTFLOWS														
Materials paid		15	15	15	38	18	19	20	21	15	15	15	15	
Wages paid		9	9	9	9	9	9	9	9	9	9	9	9	
PAYE cheque		2	2	2	2	2	2	2	2	2	2	2	2	
VAT cheque		7			7			9			9			
Rates paid					15									
Electricity			4			3			2			3		
Advertising		1	1	1	1	1	1	1	1	1	1	1	1	
Drawings		3	3	3	3	4	4	3	3	3	3	3	4	
Insurance			2			2			2			2		
Capital expenditure					63					53				
Sub-total		37	36	30	138	39	35	44	40	83	39	35	31	
Net cash flow		(7)	(4)	4	(52)	22	27	30	41		(3)	(5)	(1)	
Opening cash balance		(40)	(47)	(51)	(47)	(99)	(77)	(50)	(20)	21	21	18	13	12
Closing cash balance	(40)	(47)	(51)	(47)	(99)	(77)	(50)	(20)	21	21	18	13	12	

Cash forecasts of less than a month A monthly table does not show all the details. As a rule you will first pay your suppliers, then a week later you will receive your customer's money (if on credit terms).

This means *within one month* you can have problems, leading, possibly, to a telephone call from your bank manager!

If you can explain your firm's normal monthly pattern there will be no problem - provided there is an overall upward trend in your cash reserves.

Good cash flow management will also enable you to:

- reduce bank charges, by ensuring you fulfil the bank's requirements to avoid charges; these 'requirements' are usually not to let your balance fall below a certain amount, e.g. £50
- reduce interest charges on your overdraft by reducing the overdraft
- earn interest on any surplus cash by transferring it to a deposit account or, better still, a building society.

Some general comments about cash

Some cash is usually kept on the premises, called *petty cash* or *cash in hand.* More is usually available through a bank account.

The advantages of having your cash in a bank are, first, that the money is safer, and second, writing out cheques saves the time of counting out large numbers of notes.

The firm's cash will thus appear in the balance sheet as 'cash in hand' and 'cash in bank' among the other current assets.

Any cash kept in a bank deposit account or building society account will be subject to some withdrawal regulations. It will also be earning interest - thus, *this cash is an investment* and will appear as such among the current assets.

Cash held not earning interest is a drain on the firm. Drawing unnecessary cash from an overdraft is expensive. Also, banks do not like deposit accounts being used as current accounts. Therefore some compromise between having enough petty cash to run the firm, and not losing out on interest payments is necessary. Only *you* can decide how much cash must be held ready for immediate use.

Most bank branches are only too keen to open a current account for a local firm. You *should* find them knocking on your door. Choose the branch that offers you the largest overdraft facilities at the lowest rates, even if you do not need the overdraft now. *Remember, they make a profit even on your current account. On your overdraft they get interest payments as well.* Shop around.

Cheques

Technically, what is a cheque? It is an *instruction* to the bank to pay the person named (the *payee*), the amount stated, on the day stated. The amount is to come from the firm who signs the cheque (the *payer*, or the *drawer*). Needless to say the bank is only obliged to obey the instruction if the drawer signing the cheque has any money in that bank!

It is usually good practice for a firm's cheques to need *two* signatures. This is true even if it is only the owner-manager and a senior clerk. It reduces the risk of fraud, provides a last check that the cheque should be made out, and also ensures that more than one person is aware of the transaction.

Crossed cheques In an attempt to reduce the large amount of fraud that banks suffer, they prefer to supply 'crossed' cheques. That is, the cheque has two vertical lines through the middle of it. The effect of a crossed cheque is that normally the cheque cannot be changed for cash. If I sign a cheque, and write 'Cash' as the payee, then the bank will give me the amount stated in cash. However, if my cheques are crossed, and I write Mr Jones as the payee, the bank will not give Mr Jones the cash amount stated. The bank will pay it either into Mr Jones's account (at any bank), into a Giro account, or into any other savings account. It is possible for me to cross out the crossed lines, write 'Pay cash', and then Mr Jones will get cash.

Endorsed cheques If Mr A gives (draws) a cheque to Mr B for £50, and Mr B owes money to Mr C, Mr B can write on the back of the cheque 'Please pay Mr C', and sign this instruction. Mr C can then take this *endorsed* cheque to the bank, and they will transfer the £50 from Mr A's account to Mr C's account. If Mr A had written 'not negotiable' or 'account payee only', then Mr B could not pass it on (endorse it) to Mr C.

Cheques as receipts From the bank's point of view, cheques also act as receipts in case you challenge any withdrawals. If you pay any money into the bank, you want a receipt. The usual paying-in slip is perforated - one half the bank retains with your signature on it, the other you retain with the bank's stamp on it. Other details on the slip will be the date of paying in, the amount (in what form), the exact name of the account to receive the money, and the branch where this account exists.

Cheque clearance Remember to bank any cheques you receive DAILY.

This still means that three days will pass before your customer's bank account will be deducted. In these three days the drawer can:

- stop the cheque. If you do not know the customer make sure his account has been deducted before you release the goods. Banks will usually stop cheques right up to the moment they actually write the deduction onto the client's account.
- raise the money. Even a three days' credit period can be used wisely.
- test the goods. You can use this as a sales point. Rather than give credit so that customers can see if they like the product, say that they can always stop the cheque.

If a cheque has a bank credit card (cheque guarantee) number on the back, the cheque cannot be stopped.

Credit cards

Bank credit cards have two roles: (1) to enable you to buy on credit terms at very high interest rates, and (2) to act as a cheque guarantee. If your bank credit card number is on the back of a cheque you have signed, the bank will honour the cheque even if you do not appear to have any money with them. After honouring it they will be around to see you!

A credit card is a very small source of finance but an expensive one. You would be better off with a properly organized loan.

Book-keeping for cash

Let us consider that perfectionist amongst book-keepers, your bank and *its* accounts, one of which is you. You are one of the bank's creditors, a person the bank owes money to. (If you have an overdraft you will be the bank's debtor.) Every so often you send your customers a copy of your account on them to show them what your record says; likewise, the banks send you a copy of their account on you - they call it a *statement*, and usually send it monthly. *You should ask for them as frequently as they will agree to, even daily.* Check if you are being charged to receive statements.

Their book-keeping (debits and credits) on your account (statement) will appear to be the wrong way around. They are, to you, but not to the bank. Thus, the bank will record money you receive and pass to them for keeping as being an increase in their creditors, a credit entry. You, meanwhile, will be writing up the bank account in your general ledger with debit money received.

So your bank statement *should* be a mirror image of the bank account in your general ledger. It will never be an exact mirror image because the banks are always at least three days behind with the cheques *you* have written.

Inflation

How does inflation affect small businesses?

Inflation means increased prices, which leads to the administration costs of constantly updating prices and costings.

More important, it is a threat to your cash reserves, your liquidity. This is because not all your previous year's profit is available for drawings, paying taxes and paying for new plant. Some of your profit will have to be spent on paying the extra cost increases. During inflation it takes more and more cash just to keep the firm the same size (because of the increased costs).

Action required It is, in fact, very little more than you should be doing anyway. You should be sure that enough of your profits each year are put aside to pay for inflation. How much will depend on how much inflation you feel the firm will experience over the next year.

This is best estimated by compiling a *forecasted* profit and loss account, a balance sheet and a cash-flow forecast. When costing always use the last invoice price you paid, not what you actually paid for a particular item. Forecasts, although a problem in themselves, eliminate the problem of inflation.

Action Guidelines

1 A lack of cash will stop a firm trading. Make sure that you control your cash flow - do not let it control you.

2 A cash flow statement may well be of more use than a profit and loss account. If you make no other use of this book, at least make sure you do regular cash flow forecasts.

3 Have another look at your cash flow forecast particularly looking to see whether it can be improved by a different timing of capital expenditure.

Section 3

Management of Capital

16

Dealing with the Bank

- **Banks are a small company's primary source of money.**
- **Banks offer to small firms many services other than loans.**
- **If you borrow from a bank, what do they want to know?**
- **You must sell yourself to the bank manager.**

Bank services

What can your bank do for you? Initially it can provide the basic banking services:

- current accounts
- overdrafts
- statements of account
- bank transfers (standing orders, etc.)
- payouts in prestated denomination (for your payroll)

Then it can provide *business development loans,* between £2000 and £250,000, for one to ten years with *fixed* repayments.

Alternatively, or as well, it can provide *venture capital* - 10-year *term* loans, postponed initial repayments, fixed rates of interest. The bank can become a minority partner.

It can provide various other services, including:

- leasing and hire purchase
- payroll and accounting services
- tax advisory services
- pensions advice

- insurance advice
- sales ledger administration.

Bank managers like to think that they are *contributing* towards the firm, but you are expected to put more in than they do! At the moment banks are almost embarrassed by the high levels of their profits, so if they won't lend you *any* (no matter how nicely they put it) there is probably something wrong with your firm!

Borrowing routine

You have decided that you would like to borrow some money from your bank. How should you go about it?

First of all telephone the manager to arrange an appointment. You can offer to send him some figures before the meeting, but if you do, make sure that he receives them. He will not be impressed with your business prowess if you default on your very first promise!

When you go for the meeting remember that it is you who is the salesman - you are selling yourself and your business plan, the bank is the customer. The best way to impress the bank manager is to behave at all times like a professional - smile, wear moderate clothes and be polite.

Present your case clearly and concisely. Plan your answers and have figures to back up anything you say, where possible.

The bank manager will need to know about many aspects of your business. We shall now deal with the main ones.

You He will want to know your age, experience, education and training. He will be interested in how you became involved in your firm, and your own financial worth (house, investments and liabilities).

The firm He will want to know what it does and where, and he will be interested in its organization and accounting systems.

On the financial side he will ask you for past profit and loss accounts, balance sheets, cash flow statements, and details of drawings and profit retained.

Almost certainly he will want details of previous financial arrangements - loans, HP, leasing, etc. - and a more detailed description of your fixed assets.

The reason for the loan Your plan should include forecast cash flow figures, staff requirements and contingency plans.

Your employees You should be in a position to state their ages, experience, etc. You may well be asked whether there is a replacement for you in an emergency.

Your market Make sure you know the estimated demand, the market size, the competition, your uniqueness factors, and of course your own product details.

The amount of the loan The bank manager will want to know how much you want, in what form, and for what *exactly.* What will be your contribution, and will you want subsequent loans?

Repayment times and amounts Make sure that you can explain how you have estimated your returns, how long your operating cycle (for overdrafts) is, and what you will do if interest rates change.

Security For the bank manager these will be extremely important questions. What assets have you? What would they be worth if sold? What other loans have you on them? What personal guarantees have you to offer?

Banks are impressed by full commitment on your part (this includes offering *your* house as security, *your* money being invested and *your* relying on the business as your main source of income).

Which bank?

Shop around, go and visit a few to see how they respond to you. Decide which you want by

- the interest charges
- the bank's charges

- the size of the loan offered
- how well you get on with the bank manager.

Tell them you are optimistic and are shopping around. Banks are in fierce competition with each other. Bank managers are keen for promotion.

The Department of Industry has started a scheme whereby it will guarantee loans given by banks to small businesses, the *Government Loan Guarantee Scheme.* It is for new and existing businesses, for loans up to £75,000 on two to seven year repayment schemes. Details include:

(a) The government will cover up to 80 per cent of a loan (not overdrafts).
(b) The government charges you for the service, at a rate of three per cent of the amount guaranteed, payable quarterly in advance. There is also an initial arrangement fee.
(c) The firm must pledge all its assets as security.
(d) It is administered mainly via the bigger banks and ICFC (see Unit 17).
(e) It excludes firms in agriculture and horticulture, finance services, education firms, forestry, clubs and pubs, real estate, railways, sports firms and cultural firms, travel, medical services.

If you want more information, go and ask your bank manager.

Relationships

Banks like to know their customers. They want *more* than a straight financial deal. In fact they often become suspicious of borrowers who make *no* attempt to keep in touch.

You need a working *relationship* with your bank. It not only makes the bank manager more tolerant, it often makes him more generous! Take time out to build up a relationship with your local bank manager. He has a lot of personal discretion.

Action Guidelines

1 Consider carefully whether you want a business partner or a loan. The bank as business partner may be more flexible with repayments.

2 Make a friend of your bank manager. Keep in regular touch with him. Despite their air of impartiality bank managers do a deal of trade on the 'social nod'.

17

Evaluating Money Sources

- **Matching the use to which money is being put with the type of money being used.**
- **Is it sensible to use overdraft money to buy fixed assets?**
- **Some money is loaned with only an interest charge. Other money is loaned in return for a say in how the business is run.**
- **A measure of good money management in a firm could be the number of different sources it utilizes.**

Various sources of money

Money is available for small businesses from many directions. Your task is to decide which of these you should use.

From internal sources Look to the following: retained profits, depreciation, tax and VAT savings, reduction in drawings, improved profitability, and shortening of the operating cycle (which includes reducing the amount of debtors).

From other people Consider the following: an overdraft, bank loans, creditors, factoring, leasing (including sale and lease-back), special organization loans (including ICFC), share issue (equity), personal loans, mortgages, and hire purchase.

How do you decide?

Each source should be considered under the following heads:

(A) repayment method
(B) cost
(C) when to use that method
(D) power of loaners
(E) how it may affect later loans
(F) availability
(G) end use of money

In the following sections we shall match the source with the evaluation of it. We shall repeatedly use (A)–(G) above. First to be dealt with are the 'internal' sources.

Retained profit

(A) Repayment will come as future *increased* profits, usually in less than two years.

(B) There are *no* capital repayments, interest charges or administration charges. Using this money for investments does mean you have foregone the opportunity to earn interest on it in a deposit account.

(C) Use retained profit to finance another project whenever possible – it is the best source of cash.

(D) It is your money and you can do with it what you wish. No one will be looking over your shoulder.

(E) If later you ask for a loan, most loaners will be impressed to hear you often finance new projects by reinvesting your own profits.

(F) It is not available to new firms or firms making a loss! If this marvellous source of money is available to you, use it.

(G) Retained profit can be used to finance anything from an increase in stocks to the purchase of buildings. Because small businesses are often short of the latter (money for fixed assets) it may be well used there.

Depreciation

When you depreciate an asset you reduce the profit available for drawings. Thus your cash reserve will increase, or rather recover.

(A) The depreciation method used on your different assets will determine how much cash you are making available. We have in depreciation a sort of 'negative repayment' because depreciation starts after the purchase!
(B) There are no obvious costs to using depreciation.
(C) This method should be considered as building up a reserve of cash (by reducing your profit figure) to replace the fixed asset.
(D) Like all internal sources of finance there is no problem of having to consider loaners' actions.
(E) Later loans are not affected.
(F) It is available to anyone depreciating assets.
(G) Depreciation should be used to replace the asset it refers to. Usually these days it is not enough owing to rising prices. In this case you can depreciate on the replacement cost of the asset.

Tax (including VAT) provisions

It may seem strange to think of tax as a loan, but you do get use of this liability for some months.

(A) You will have to repay in a large lump, so have the money available at the repayment time.
(B) There is no cost, unless you upset the taxman by paying him back too late. Then the cost may be your firm, or interest.
(C) This provision, like any creditor, should be used to maximum advantage all the time.
(D) The taxman will not interfere with your management of the firm. The situation is black and white to him – you pay and he stays away. You *don't* pay and he shuts you down.
(E) If you delay or default on a tax payment, later lenders will take a very dim view of it.
(F) It is only available provided you earn profits to pay tax on or if you are VAT registered.
(G) The money should only be used to finance very short-term (near cash) assets like debtors and finished goods stock.

Reduced drawings

If your firm has cash problems the first move must be to pay yourself less!

(A) There will be complete flexibility of *how* and *when* you decide to later draw the money.
(B) There are no costs.
(C) This is a method of 'first action'. Use it prior to going to a bank. You should, however, make good use of bank money to run your business.
(D) There are no lenders to consider.
(E) Your self-sacrifice will impress other lenders.
(F) The amount loaned by the firm will clearly vary by how much drawings you can afford not to take. If there are no profits you cannot take any drawings anyway.
(G) Drawings unclaimed would usually be used to pay for short-term assets, e.g. stocks and debtors. If you do not intend to take the drawings for some years, longer-term assets can be purchased with the money now available.

Improved profitability

This will entail selling more, reducing costs or increasing the selling price.

(A) Eventually any increase in profit will have to be paid out to the owners as drawings.
(B) There are no direct costs, but this increased profitability may be at some expense.
(C) Needless to say, use this method if and when possible.
(D) There are no lenders to consider.
(E) Again this improved profitability will impress investors.
(F) Clearly it is easier to say than do, especially in the short term.
(G) The cash could be used to finance long-term assets.

Improved operating cycle

This includes cutting down the period between when you pay for goods and when you receive the cash for sales.

(A) There is no question of repayment here unless some of the measures are only temporary.
(B) It costs nothing, in fact interest on loans may be saved.
(C) Reducing the operating cycle to its *optimum*, thus minimizing the cash used, should be a constant management task.
(D) There is no question of other lenders.
(E) It will impress investors later.
(F) Such a source of cash is usually available to most firms. Often more incentives to staff can improve the 'cycle'.
(G) This money must only be used to pay for short-term assets.

Overdraft

(A) Repayment is automatic with each cash payment received. These reduce the loan.
(B) The interest rates are high. This percentage is, however, only on the balance outstanding.
(C) Overdrafts should be one of your first *external* sources of cash. Do not use it for everything – it is costly but it is flexible.
(D) The bank will not get involved with day-to-day management, but if they decide (as they often do) to reduce the size of your overdraft limit you have to jump. They are also experts at closing down small businesses.
(E) A large, badly administered, overdraft will cause you problems in raising other types of loans. Remember you need a mix of types of loans.
(F) Overdrafts are fairly readily available from local banks if you are willing to pay the rates.
(G) Overdraft money must be used only to finance stocks and debtors.

Bank loans

(A) The repayments of interest plus capital are usually deducted by standing order, monthly. Interest is on the balance calculated daily. The repayment period must be agreed before the loan is given, between two and five years.
(B) You have to pay the interest rate.

(C) Again it should be one of your first *external* sources of cash, but unlike overdrafts this is for more fixed assets.

(D) Remember banks are experts at closing down firms. As long as they get paid they will not interfere in the firm.

(E) If you repay your first loan properly the chances of a second loan are high.

(F) The availability of bank loans does depend on the government rules on the supply of cash, but usually some bank will have money to lend. It is how they make a living.

(G) This money can be used to buy fixed assets which are expected to pay for themselves within a short time period.

Creditors

Buying on credit is just the same as a one-month loan.

(A) Repayment is the entire sum in one lump when due. Good management will be able to delay payment without upsetting suppliers.

(B) Whilst *normally* there is no interest charge, the friendship of your supplier is at risk if you extend the loan beyond the normal period. If you forego a settlement discount because you are not ready to pay, this may be considered the cost of the loan.

(C) This is a very useful cheap source of cash. You should make maximum use of it continually.

(D) Creditors are often reluctant to put customers in court. This is partly because of the costs involved, and partly because they will have little experience in legal matters. The county court system for small debts has improved creditors' power of recovering debts.

(E) If your creditors start saying you are a bad payer it may affect later attempts to raise money elsewhere.

(F) Most firms give the normal one-month's credit on supplies. It helps *their* administration, as well as yours. A good firm will give you a hard time if you take more than the agreed credit period. If supplies are scarce a supplier who has you noted as a bad payer may disrupt your deliveries.

(G) This money must only be used to finance your credit sales. If you have things well worked out, your debtors will be paid for by your creditors – the amounts will balance out.

Factoring

You can sell some of your debtors to a 'factor' for cash *now*. Usually the person buying your debtors will advance you about 75 per cent of the sales ledger value in the same month as the sale. The remaining 25 per cent you get when the debtors pay up. This 'factor' also takes a commission for himself, and he may also want interest on the 75 per cent loan.

The advantages are that you get your cash now, and there is no sales ledger collection administration to pay for.

The *disadvantages* are that the discretion of when to take a debtor to court moves to someone else; and that it may confuse your customers, buying from you and paying the factor.

(A) The factor repays you 75 per cent on sale date, 25 per cent on payment date.
(B) The costs equal (1) the factor's commission, (2) the factor's interest charge, (3) lost customers' goodwill. But you will save some time in collecting debts.
(C) Use factoring when you have no time or skill at debt collection, you have a large or complex ledger, or when you have insensitive customers.
(D) The factor has complete power of how to collect debts.
(E) It is hard to say how banks will react to factoring. Some think it is a good idea, others will like you to show you can do it yourself. The banks do offer a factoring service.
(F) Finding someone to 'take on' your sales ledger should not be too hard provided you have a *good* record with your debt collection. They will not take a ledger to *save* a firm in a cash crisis.
(G) This money should be used only to repay creditors.

Leasing

(A) Repayment is in the form of rentals, usually paid quarterly over two to five years. Then you might renew the lease (a secondary lease) on a nominal rental.

(B) Leasing rentals can be high, and you never actually own the asset. The rentals are a company expense and so reduce the firm's tax bill on its profits. Be wary of salesmen who quote rentals less tax. It's not wrong (if you are making profits to be taxed) but is a bit confusing. You should cost a lease by adding up the rentals.

(C) Leasing is a good way of getting fixed assets (especially those that need maintenance or get out of date quickly) when you do not have the cash. It does mean you do not own the asset but often that does not really matter. Leasing is often used after you have exhausted loans but a comparison of the costs (after tax) of *both* must be made. Do not lease an asset likely to increase in value.

(D) The leasing companies do not usually bother you about how you use the asset leased but sometimes want to know where it is or what condition it is in. If you default on the rentals they will sue for the balance of the rentals as well as collect their asset.

(E) Provided you can repay the rentals future loans will not be affected. *Assets leased do not appear on your balance sheet (they are not yours).* The leased asset is its own security.

(F) Leasing is easy enough - there are many leasing companies. The rental you pay will depend on how risky the leasing company think you are. They measure this risk by looking at your previous year's profit record.

(G) When leasing you get the asset, not the money to buy the asset. You lease fixed assets, not stocks and debtors.

Sale and leaseback

Here, for example, you *sell* your factory to a leasing company which leases it back to you for a quarterly rental. This means that you do not have all your cash tied up in buildings. This is true with all leases.

The decision should be based on your being confident that you can earn a rate of profit greater than the increase in the building value.

Remember that when the lease runs out you may be thrown out! This could be acceptable if you wanted bigger or better premises anyway.

Some entrepreneurs make good use of sale-and-leaseback. They find companies for sale where the sale value to them is *below* the asset value. The asset value is what you would get on a 'sale-and-leaseback' agreement. They buy, then 'sale-and-leaseback' the assets (including buildings), thus showing a profit. They still have the firm (leased) so they can *also* make a profit by normal trading!

How (you should be asking) can the sale price of a firm be below its asset value? It can be so if it is a 'public' company where the market value of all its shares (certificates sold in return for a part ownership in a firm) is less than the firm's asset value, due to market demand being poor or the shareholders' lack of faith in the directors.

Special organization loans

These include finance from the Industrial and Commercial Finance Corporation (ICFC), local authority loans, tourist boards, large companies' pension funds, and many more.

(A) These are usually fixed-interest loans repayable monthly or quarterly.
(B) The cost will often be slightly above the bank loan rate.
(C) The use of this money is for fixed assets. If the bank is not interested in your firm (beyond an overdraft for stock and debtors) then you should turn to these firms. Check their rates against the bank's.
(D) Whilst the lenders of debt finance like this do not usually get involved in the day-to-day management of the firm, they will not like not being repaid on time! Some of them do actually require part ownership of the firm before they will lend you money.
(E) These lenders will most likely want to secure their loan against your assets. It is usual to have a debt capacity of 50 to 60 per cent of your asset value. If all your assets have prior charges (rights) on them, later loans may be hard to arrange.

(F) These loans should be available to you. You will, however, have to prove you have a healthy respect for accounting records and methods, like a cash flow forecast.

(G) This money is usually for fixed assets.

Share issue

This means that you allow other people to buy in as part owners. If you put in £10,000 and they put in £10,000, you would be equal owners with equal say in how to run the firm. This type of money is called 'equity capital'. Private individuals, banks and loan companies sometimes offer equity capital.

(A) Repayment to the supplier of equity capital is via either (*a*) annual dividends – these are a portion of the profits (as you decide fair), or (*b*) by being able to sell all or part of their share in ownership of the firm to someone else at a profit.

(B) Cost (apart from lost ownership and freedom of action) is the dividend. This is usually larger than the interest payment on a loan of equivalent size.

(C) You would use equity when (*a*) you could get none other, or (*b*) you wanted a partner (e.g. a bank's expertise), or (*c*) when you knew your profit was liable to large fluctuations. With fixed regular interest charges default on one payment may lead to closure. With dividends you can decide *when* you want to pay. You may pay nothing one year and a double amount the next.

(D) With equity the owners can tell you how to run the firm. They may be able to sell out their part of the firm to anyone. If they do not like the dividend they will not usually close you down though.

(E) As the division of loans (debt) and equity is usually around 50/50 in the UK, if you take on equity you can often later get loans.

(F) Equity is available but usually, again, providers of equity (shareholders) will demand good accounting records. The question you must ask yourself is whether you *want* a partner.

(G) The money should be used to buy fixed assets.

Private loans

You may be able to get relatives, neighbours and local businessmen to lend you money.

(A) Repayment will have to be clearly stated. The interest rate and the dates for repayment of interest and capital will need to be written down and signed. Get it witnessed by a solicitor.
(B) The cost will vary, but in order for an individual to forego the safe return of a bank deposit account they will need a good rate of return.
(C) Use this method when all else fails, unless you can (for some reason) get favourable terms. Remember individuals are less competent in closing firms down.
(D) The power, therefore, of lenders to close you down exists but is considerably weaker than for banks, etc.
(E) It should not affect later loans.
(F) Such money is available. Ask around. It is not unknown for people to advertise their need for private money.
(G) The time the loan is for will determine if you should spend it on current assets or fixed assets.

Mortgages

(A) Repayment is of both interest and capital in monthly instalments over 10 to 25 years.
(B) It is usually a cheap source of money. The interest rates do fluctuate during the loan period.
(C) Mortgages are mainly used for building loans. You get to own the building.
(D) The mortgagers can reclaim their building if you default on payment. They hold the deeds.
(E) It will not usually affect later loans.
(F) Mortgages are available through banks, building societies and special mortgage loan companies.
(G) This money is for buying buildings, mainly.

Hire purchase

(A) Repayment is of a monthly or quarterly payment over 2–3 years.

(B) As you pay interest on the initial sum it is usually an expensive loan system. You get capital allowance (i.e. taxman's depreciation) on the asset rather than being allowed to charge the payments as expenses.

(C) It should be used when you want to own the asset and cannot get any other loan.

(D) The HP company will reclaim the asset if you default on payment but will not worry what you are doing with the asset.

(E) The HP company has prior charge on the asset, so it will not be so easy to offer the asset as security against later loans.

(F) HP is available if you have a good 'track record'. It is not a popular form of finance for firms.

(G) This money is, of course, used to buy fixed assets.

Action Guidelines

1 Since the method used to finance the purchase of an asset should relate to the type of asset and to the owner's needs, it is normal to see, in a well run business, a good mixture of methods. Have the right *financial package.* Do not use an overdraft for everything, especially as banks can reduce overdraft limits at very short notice to suit their own needs.

2 Make sure you are aware of the proportion of finance that you are getting from internal sources.

18

Drawings and Valuations

- **Profits are used to repay the owners for their efforts, to provide money for growth, and to provide money to pay for increased costs due to inflation.**
- **Overdrawing kills firms. An owner's wealth is increased by his drawings *and* any increase in the valuation of the firm.**
- **Knowing about valuations allows you to bargain hunt for firms or make a good sale.**

Drawings are any expense paid by the firm to the owner's personal financial advantage.

Good management of your drawings is essential for maximizing your wealth and the firm's cash flow.

Drawings include a salary, private mileage in a company car, entertainment, personal telephone bills, use of company labour on private work and any issues from stock. If you pay a wife or close relative, this also is drawings.

Taxes

You have to pay Schedule D income tax on all your drawings.

First your personal allowance will be deducted (you're allowed that much before the taxing starts). The rest will be taxed, the present level being a basic 30 per cent.

There are five types of tax that will affect you and your business.

Income Tax This is paid on *your* drawings.

Corporation Tax This is paid on the profit your firm makes before drawings. It is 40 per cent of net profit if the profit is less than £80,000, 52 per cent of net profit if the profit is more than £200,000 and between 40 and 52 per cent (on a sliding scale) for those in between.

This net profit is after deducting the taxman's rates of depreciation, and his allowances for the effect of inflation on your stock levels.

Capital Gains Tax This is a tax on any increase in value of an asset. It is a form of income tax, where your income is your increased wealth.

Capital Transfer Tax This is a tax on any large 'gifts' of money you transfer to someone else. It was designed to beat death duty 'avoiders'.

VAT This was a replacement for (and massive increase in) purchase tax. It is administered by Customs and Excise, not the Inland Revenue. It was designed partly to discourage excessive cost increases caused by middle-men.

You and your firm will pay tax, but each are allowed *expenses.* For the firm, these are materials and overheads; for you, these could be (at the taxman's discretion) a portion of your mortgage, electricity bill, telephone bill, furniture, etc. if you can establish that you use your home to handle business matters.

Tax is an especially complicated thing – you will need a tax adviser for specific advice. It is a cost that must be properly managed – an important management task is to recruit a good tax adviser.

If your firm is limited (that is, the total liability of the owners is limited to their initial investment only), then instead of 'drawings' the terminology used is usually 'distributions' or 'dividends'. For every £70 you withdraw from the firm, it will have to pay tax of £30 (i.e. 30 per cent of £100). This £30 tax is called Advance Corporation Tax (ACT). When the limited company's profits are taxed, it can reclaim any ACT it has paid out.

There is *no* tax advantage to getting the firm to pay your bills. In fact there are disadvantages:

- there is extra administration for the firm
- you may overdraw by mistake

Overdrawing

Do not bleed your potentially successful company dry. Many small businessmen have. Do not even do it by mistake!

You should

- intend to pay yourself a fixed sum each month and year-end bonus on profit
- base this sum on profits earned *and* retained last year
- first check that the firm has the money available as cash, not as stocks or debtors
- choose carefully the time in the month you take the money – don't take it when you are in the middle of paying a lot of creditors
- keep your's and the firm's finances as separate as possible, including bank accounts – this will save you accountants' fees and surprise tax statements!
- keep (if you must have non-salary drawings) a good clear 'drawings account' in your general ledger
- use your cash flow forecast to adjust your drawings as necessary.

Retained profit

The people who lend you money will expect you to show some commitment to the future growth of the firm. They will expect you to:

(a) reinvest around two-thirds of each year's profit back into the firm

(b) finance a large part of your firm's expansion programme from retained profit
(c) be able to identify clearly where you used the retained profit – that is, as working capital or as fixed assets.

When loans are advanced, they usually only represent about half of the money needed to finance the firm. The other half comes from you (capital) and your retained profit.

Thus the ratio of *your* money to *loans* will be 1 to 1; that is your *gearing ratio* will be 1 to 1.

If half the money invested is yours, and half the bank's, this means that half your assets' value will have loans against it. Half is a reasonable figure. If (after retaining profit for a while) the proportion of your assets financed by loans drops below 50 per cent, you have some spare DEBT CAPACITY.

Your debt capacity is how much more you can borrow by giving your assets as security.

The firm can increase *your* wealth two ways:

- via income (salary)
- by increased value

It is therefore in your interest to know the value of your firm.

Valuing a small firm

There are a few calculative methods for valuing firms. It is, however, important to bear in mind that value is subjective. No matter what the figures say, you may be unwilling to part with your firm for less than a certain figure. Whether a buyer is willing to pay this depends on how badly he wants the firm. Calculations can only be a guide to a firm's value. We shall now look at some of the calculative methods.

Asset value Here you forget the balance sheet. You try to get an independent valuation on all the firm's cars, lorries, machines, buildings, etc. as if you were selling them off separately. The best definite prices would be totalled to value the firm. Do not forget to deduct the liabilities.

Profits You first take the average net profits after tax for the last five years. Next you ask yourself what return (after tax) you would get if you invested £100 in a building society. Add 20 per cent to this for the risk. Next, capitalize your profit using this risk-return percentage.

Here is an example:

After-tax net profit 5 years ago		= £40,000
,,	4 years ,,	= £45,000
,,	3 years ,,	= £43,000
,,	2 years ,,	= £47,000
,,	1 year ,,	= £49,000
		£224,000

Average profit	= £44,800
Building society interest (after tax)	= 9%
Add 20%	= 29%
Value of firm	$= \dfrac{£44{,}800}{29\%}$
	= £154,482

Assets value plus five years' excess profit Suppose that the owners agree that you might want 29 per cent (above) but every other firm in the same industry only earns around 24 per cent.

Further suppose that you have had the firm's assets valued at £165,926. This would make *this* firm's returns $\dfrac{£44{,}800}{£165{,}926} = 27\%$

Hence:

		£
Normal profits	= 24% × £165,926 =	39,822 per year
This firm's profit	= 27% × £165,926 =	44,800 per year
	Difference =	4,978
For five years =		× 5
		£24,890

The value of this firm is therefore

Asset value =	165,926
Five years' excess profit =	24,890
	£190,816

The use of five years is conventional only. Now if you bought this firm, your balance sheet would show:

Capital	190,816	Goodwill	24,890
		Assets	165,926
	£190,816		£190,816

Action Guidelines

1 Tax is a manageable cost. Get an expert to manage it.

2 If your firm is doing well but you do not want to take out too much in drawings, you should consider taking out a personal loan (against the firm's assets).

3 The usefulness of understanding valuation is that you can seek a bargain company to buy out. You will also know how much of a bargain your firm might be to a larger organization!

4 *Your* wealth is in your firm. You must be careful to keep a check on what you are worth. This worth can be increased or decreased by:

(*a*) profit from trading
(*b*) profit from increasing values of assets.

19

Conclusions

Let us remind ourselves why accountancy has become so integrated into business life. Because *it provides information.* Information about the financial performance of the firm.

It is only one source of information. The other sources, like customers' and competitors' reactions, are equally vital to the success of a firm.

Accounting and financial management must then be woven into the existing organization BUT must *not* become an end in itself.

One big advantage of accounting is that it *can* be used to see the end effect of a manager's decisions. You feel, say, that customers are reacting favourably to the new finish on your product, or the new presentation of your service. Is that reaction significant enough to offset the expenses incurred? Or, just how much difference did that reaction affect the standard of living of the owner? Accountancy can tell you.

To sum up

- The units on keeping accounting records will provide you with a recognized method of recording your transactions and debts.
- The units on calculating your monthly profit and loss account and balance sheet will let you know how well you are doing.
- The unit on ratio analysis will show you how your creditors (including banks) will view your firm. They will be concerned to see not only what your profit is but also if you have sufficient capital to trade at the present level. That is, they will be checking that you are not overtrading.

- The unit on costing showed you the two basic ways of costing products - one for the production company, the other for a jobbing company. Both avoided overhead apportionment.
- The unit on pricing pointed out the need to see your product as your customers would. You should be flexible in your pricing, you should clearly identify your competitive advantage (e.g. convenience) and advertise it. Your main question in pricing should be, 'at that price *how many* must I sell to achieve my required profit?'
- The unit on buying fixed assets pointed out that you must first identify the important variable in your purchase (e.g. petrol, electricity, volume of output). Then compare the cost of that against the different initial costs. You should also consider the payback period. You should assume you had to borrow in order to pay for the asset. Thus the cost includes interest.
- The unit on banks and sources of finance pointed out that (1) you must match your use of money with its source; (2) you should have a 'financial package', not just an overdraft; (3) you should build up a good relationship with your bank manager and fully use the bank's range of facilities.
- The units on planning (including cash) pointed out the need for information about the future as much as of the past. Such information is demanded by lenders and may save you a lot of time and money later. You cannot manage without forecasting.

Final comments

Your product or service and your character are your vehicles to success. Accounting and finance management are your dashboard, *USE IT.* Most small businesses fail through poor money management - will yours?

If the book was too simple for *your* needs then look at the suggested reading list.

If you disagreed with parts of the book, that is good. You have at least thought about the problem. It is your firm so do as you wish.

You should have a hundred unanswered, detailed questions. That, too, is good. The book cannot answer *every* question. Note these questions and *find* the answers.

We recommend that you should now try the self-help checklist which follows.

Self-help Checklist

1 What is capital?
2 Are your ledgers kept up to date?
3 Do you prepare monthly accounts?
4 Have you prepared a budget?
5 Have you prepared cash budgets?
6 Have you a system for finding out WHY your customers buy from YOU?
7 Can you specify your break-even volumes?
8 Are you suffering from overstocking, too long a working capital cycle or overdrawing?
9 Have you identified in your monthly accounts any ratios that suggest a need for corrective action?
10 Do you know whether your firm is about to have a cash flow crisis?
11 Do you provide funds in a bank deposit account or otherwise, by way of saving towards your tax on profits?
12 Have you specified levels for your raw materials stocks?
13 Do you ask all new credit customers to submit to formal vetting procedures?
14 Is the difference between the credit period stated in your Conditions of Trading and the days' sales shown by your ratio analysis less than 15 days?
15 Do you adhere to a preset target for your personal drawings throughout the year?
16 Have you recently reviewed your fixed overheads item by item with a view to curbing their growth?
17 Have you taken steps to familiarize yourself with the requirements of the laws on VAT?
18 Do you know which elements of working capital are principally responsible for the length of your operating cycle?
19 Do you keep checks on the staff who handle your cash?
20 How will you finance your next purchase – by loan, by overdraft or from creditors?

Some Useful Addresses

A book containing very many useful addresses is *The Directory of Sources of Information and Advice* (for new and small businesses), available from the B.B.C. or

Colin Barrow
Director
Small Business Unit
Thames Polytechnic
School of Business Administration
Riverside House
London SE18 6EU

This directory contains details of grants, leasing companies, useful publications, useful libraries, small business centres, courses, lenders, factoring companies, premises, market information, government bodies, etc.

The telephone book 'commercial classified directory' has a lot of useful local addresses. On looking through the northern area book I have seen addresses for:

Accommodation agencies - business
Suppliers and potential customers
Business consultants
Data processing services (computer bureaux)
Debt collectors
Export agents
Factoring
Finance companies (including ICFC)

For copies of a company's accounts:

Companies House
55 City Road
London EC1 Tel: 01-253 9393

For more details of the accounts of companies in the same industry as you:

The Centre for Interfirm Comparison
25 Bloomsbury Square
London WC1A 2PT   Tel: 01-637 8404

and

Inter Company Comparison
81 City Road
London EC1Y 1BD   Tel: 01-251 4941

For government publications:

Her Majesty's Stationery Office
PO Box 569
London WC1 9N4   Tel: 01-928 6977

and

The Small Firms Division
Department of Industry
Abell House
John Islip Street
London SW1P 4LN

For advice on how to import a car, and on consumer laws:

Consumers' Association
14 Buckingham Street
London WC2N 6DS   Tel: 01-839 1222

Useful local services for information include:

your library
your technical college or polytechnic and their libraries
the Town Hall
your bank!

Pamphlets, publications and forms for PAYE and VAT include:

Leaflet P7	*Employers' guide to PAYE*
Various	Tax tables and forms for operating PAYE
Leaflet NP15	*Employers' guide to National Insurance contributions*
Leaflet CA1	*Capital allowances on machinery or plant*

Leaflet IR9	*Notes on the treatment of livestock kept by farmers and other traders*
Leaflet IR11	*Tax treatment of interest paid*
Leaflet NI41	*National Insurance guidance for the self-employed*
Leaflet NP18	*Class 4 National Insurance contributions*
Leaflet IR24	*Class 4 National Insurance contributions: Memorandum on the computation of profits*
Leaflet IR14/15	*Construction industry: Tax deduction scheme explanatory booklet for contractors and sub-contractors*
Leaflet CGT8	*Capital Gains Tax*
700	*General guide*

All these are freely available from the appropriate government department.

Recommended Further Reading

After The Abacus, W. Harper

A Practical Guide to Good Book-keeping and Business Systems, John Kellock (Business Books)

Business Accounts, Frank Wood (Polytech Publishers)

Cost Accounting, W. M. Harper (M & E Handbooks)

Finance for Non-Accountants, L. E. Rockley (Business Books)

How to Understand and Use Company Accounts, Roy Warren (Business Books)

Managing Tax in Your Business, Robert Walters (Business Books)

The Management of Business Finance, John Freear (Pitman Books)

The Daily Mail Income Tax Guide, Daily Mail

The Meaning of Balance Sheets and Company Reports, L. E. Rockley (Business Books)

VAT General Guide, Customs & Excise

Starting in Business (P7), Inland Revenue

Index